GROTZ'S 2ND

ANTIQUE FURNITURE
STYLE & PRICE GUIDE

Books by George Grotz

FROM GUNK TO GLOW

THE FURNITURE DOCTOR

THE NEW ANTIQUES

ANTIQUES YOU CAN DECORATE WITH

INSTANT FURNITURE REFINISHING

STAINING AND REFINISHING UNFINISHED FURNITURE
    AND OTHER NAKED WOODS

DECORATING FURNITURE WITH A LITTLE BIT OF CLASS

THE ANTIQUE RESTORER'S HANDBOOK

THE CURRENT ANTIQUE FURNITURE STYLE & PRICE GUIDE

THE FUN OF REFINISHING FURNITURE

GROTZ'S 2ND ANTIQUE FURNITURE STYLE & PRICE GUIDE

GROTZ'S 2ND

ANTIQUE FURNITURE STYLE & PRICE GUIDE

With Decorative Accessories
French · English · American · Oriental

Edited by *GEORGE GROTZ*

AUTHOR OF *THE FURNITURE DOCTOR*

DOLPHIN BOOKS, DOUBLEDAY AND COMPANY, GARDEN CITY, NEW YORK 1982

ACKNOWLEDGMENTS

I would like to thank the following people for the use of their photographs and the wealth of information they shared with me.

Mr. David Goldberg of Morton's Auction Exchange, 643 Magazine Street, New Orleans, Louisiana 70901. (Illustrated catalogues announcing future auctions available on request.)

Mr. Robert L. Jenkins of Leonard's Antiques, just outside of Providence, Rhode Island on Route 44 going east. Mailing address: Leonard's Antiques, 600 Taunton Avenue, Seekonk, Massachusetts. (Free illustrated folder featuring Early-American beds.) Summer branch store in Newport, Rhode Island.

Mr. Charles W. Clements of Clements Antiques of Texas, Inc., located on I-20 just east of Dallas, Texas. Mailing address: P.O. Box 727, Forney, Texas 75126. (Illustrated catalogues of future auctions available on request.)

Mr. James Julia of Julia's Auction Barn, Fairfield, Maine 04937. (Illustrated catalogues of future auctions available on request.)

Mr. Richard W. Withington of Richard W. Withington, Inc., Hillsboro, New Hampshire 03244. (Illustrated catalogue announcing future auctions available on request.)

And finally, Mr. Paul Koch of the Koch Studios, Box 1, Provincetown, Massachusetts 02657. Mr. Koch acted as photographic advisor on this *2nd Antique Furniture Style & Price Guide*.

Library of Congress Cataloging in Publication Data

Grotz, George.
Grotz's 2nd antique furniture style & price guide.

A companion volume to The current antique furniture
style & price guide.
1. Furniture—England—Catalogues. 2. Furniture—France
—Catalogues. 3. Furniture—United States—Catalogues.
I. Title. II. Title: Antique furniture style & price guide.
NK2547.G73   749′.1′0750973
AACR2
ISBN: 0-385-17426-8
Library of Congress Catalog Card Number 81–43105

CONTENTS

Antiques You Can Decorate With
AND HOW WE PICKED AND PRICED THEM

I'm getting awfully tired of reading in the newspapers about block-front desks selling for $125,000 and all that jazz. And how the only antiques to buy are the very best of their kind. That's fine if your great-grandfather was named Ford or Rockefeller or DuPont. But how about the rest of us?

So that's who this book is for: us poor but gentle, cultured folk with an interest in the past—and in the artifacts of it that tell us where we came from, and what our ancestors were like, and what they accomplished . . . and what they dreamed.

And what a wild and wonderful variety these antiques come in, these antiques we can *afford* to buy and live with. These antiques we can *afford* to decorate with.

But now I can hear someone in the front row saying, "Oh, that's all fine, George, but how do we know that this is a representative selection of currently available antiques? And how do we know the prices are right?"

Well, I'm glad you asked those questions, because they give me a chance to explain how this guide was compiled.

To begin with, we went to five of the country's largest and most active auction houses operating around the country so that we would have a cross section of the American marketplace. (As opposed to the high-priced international market served by the big auction houses in New York City.)

Then at these five major sources for realistically priced antiques, we looked at their files of photographs of things they had sold in the preceding year. This established what kind of pieces were actually currently available. Altogether, we looked at some five thousand photographs, because these auction houses advertise their sales with photographs every week.

Then with the help of the managers of these auction houses we selected a thousand of the most interesting and popular pieces. These were organized with captions, and just before publication we returned to the five auction houses to get last-minute estimates of these pieces' current value in the marketplace. No computers—just the seasoned wisdom of five of the most knowledgeable men in the antiques business today.

Now, I hear someone else asking, "But wouldn't it be more useful if you gave us the retail prices in antique shops?"

And my answer is, "No." For three reasons . . .

1. All antique dealers are incurable optimists, or they wouldn't be in the business, and the prices they think they can get for things are often pure pipe dreams.

2. When a dealer isn't sure of what something is worth, he prices it very high so that he can find out through talking to customers and other dealers what they think it is worth.

3. Dealers often overprice their items as a form of sucker bait: If you show the slightest interest in something, they can quickly increase your interest by offering it to you at a much lower "bargain" price.

So competitive bidding at auctions is where reality is established, and the managers of auction houses are immersed in it every day of their lives. (They can also discount overbidding or items going too low because everybody has run out of money at the end of a sale.)

As to establishing a fair retail or antique-shop price, all you have to do is the following: For large pieces, such as sideboards and highboys, double the auction prices given in this book. This is because large pieces take up a lot of space and move slowly—thus costing the dealer a lot of overhead. For small pieces only add 50 percent because they don't take up much room and move the fastest. And for pieces in between, it's a sliding scale.

Happy hunting . . .

George Grotz

Advertising

Framed poster depicting The Great White Fleet (U.S.) for an insurance company.
$400

Advertising broadside for steamship company.
$450

De Laval advertising sign in mint condition.
$750

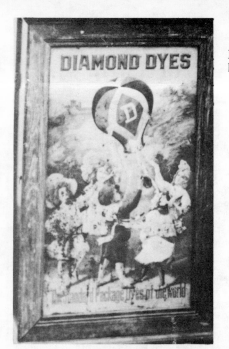

Diamond Dye counter cabinet with lithographed tin front.
$250

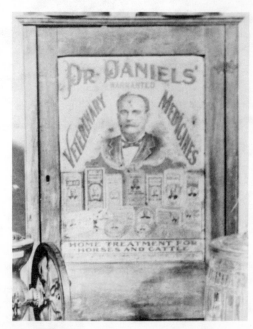

Paper silent-movie poster.
$150

Coke tray depicting "Betty," lithograph on tin.
$125

Dr. Daniels' tin-front counter cabinet.
$350

Sulky racing poster.
$400

Tin advertising sign depicting the great John L. Sullivan for a beer company. In original oak frame, 3 feet high.
$1,000

Litho on paper in excellent condition behind glass in frame for Schlitz.
$1,000

11

Cardboard trans-Atlantic advertising sign in frame.
$100

Whiskey advertising tin tray with lithograph of dogs.
$300

Emerson advertising sign, reverse printing on glass, in perfect condition.
$1,000

Cardboard Moxie sign.
$65

12

How to Buy at an Auction

Yes, Virginia, there *are* ways you can be a better bidder at auctions—which means buying things cheaper and seldom getting stung.

Rule 1: Attend the preview of the auction so you can decide at your leisure which pieces you really want to bid on. Then inspect those pieces for repairs—and think over how much restoration will cost you in time or money.

Rule 2: At the preview, make an absolutely definite decision about the top price you will pay for an item. One slip, and auction fever will destroy you.

Rule 3: At the preview, notice if there is more than one of a category of item. If there are six similar drop-leaf tables, the last is virtually certain to go cheaper than the first.

Rule 4: Always wait for the bitter end of an auction. Bring a thermos and sandwiches. Things always go cheaper when most of the ready cash has been spent, the dealers already have all that will fit in their trucks, and the auctioneer is tired and wants to go to bed.

Rule 5: Don't up the top price you will pay just because everybody is bidding higher than you. That doesn't mean they know something you don't. Hysteria sweeps auctions all the time. Those other people aren't smarter than you. You're just the only sane person on a ship of fools. Or I guess I mean, you're the only one who can see that the king has no clothes on.

Americana

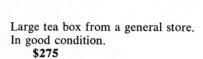
Nest of Shaker-type boxes that are always sought after. Depending on size . . .
$75–$175

Large tea box from a general store. In good condition.
$275

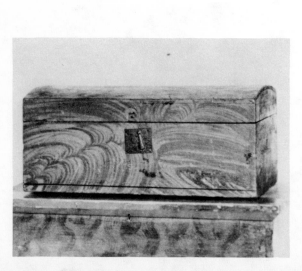

Paint-decorated pine, dovetailed document box, 2 feet long.
$275

Dome-topped traveling chest about 2½ feet long with lock and decoration.
$75

Pine salt box with drawer below. Early 1700s.
$350

Dog-power treadle machine.
$450

Polychrome decorated sailor's ditty box.
$175

Green-decorated, early 6-board
dovetailed chest.
$300

Decorated, dovetailed, 6-board
chest.
$250

Chopping bowl with plenty of
chopping marks. Maple.
$75

Chopping bowl about 2½ feet
long. Hardwood.
$55

16

Oblong chopping bowl hewn out of
solid piece of hardwood.
$75

Early blown-copper horse weather
vane, signed Cushman & Whiting.
$450

Sheet-metal horse weather vane.
$225

Primitive wooden fish weather
vane.
$250

17

Early blown-copper horse weather vane.
$350

Sheet-metal horse weather vane.
$750

Folk-Art horse weather vane.
$450

Wooden chicken weather vane
with wrought-iron brace.
$250

Sheet-metal whale weather vane.
$350

Copper weather vane of a sailing vessel.
$300

Cow weather vane of molded copper.
$750

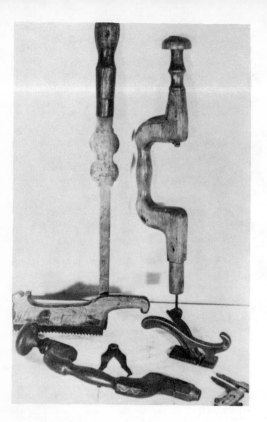

Set of early American tools with
engraved name of original owner,
circa 1790. Saw, **$250;** wooden
bitbraces, **$35;** calipers in shape of
woman's legs, **$125.**

Primitive carved-pine grain shovel,
red paint.
$300

Carved wooden grain shovel.
$225

20

Large cobbler's bench with numerous drawers.
$900
Brass-and-copper bedpans with pieced tops.
$400 and **$250**

Early pine cobbler's bench.
$250

Rough but interesting cobbler's bench once used on a farm but destined to end up as a coffee table. In the rough . . .
$350

Early cobbler's bench in old blue paint.
$750
Hewing adzes . . .
$75–$200

Group of butter stamps.
Cat-o'-nine-tails, **$150**; pineapple,
$50; swan, **$165.**

Group of butter stamps. Eagle, **$175**;
half-pound cow molds, **$150**;
berry stamp in center, **$250**;
large six-part mold behind it
with blueberries and acorns, **$150.**

Decorated tin fire horn.
$375

Fire bucket kept under the stairs
in the olden times. Now leaded for
stability and made into a lamp . . .
$185

22

Fireman's hat from Victorian
era.
$125

Early carved Folk Art, paint in
excellent condition. Done in Maine
in early 1900s by noted carver.
$1,100

School bell made in early 1900s,
brass and hardwood.
$125

Turtle-shaped bellows for use at
fireplace, original decoration.
$175

Wooden bootjack that hung by the fireplace in the keeping room. Nice old paint.
$25

Child's wheelbarrow, all original.
$135

Of course, you can put magazines in them, but you trip over the rockers all the time.
$200

Three-legged chopping block that doesn't wobble. From an old country store.
$85

24

Child's toy buckboard, circa 1900.
$500

Baby carriage from turn of the century.
$350

Canvas-covered baby carriage from about 1890. With original decoration.
$350

Wicker baby carriage, circa 1910.
$450

Surry-top baby carriage.
$375

Two-door, cut-under buggy in
pristine condition.
$3,200

Depending on the quality of the
workmanship and condition,
handmade quilts like this can run
from $200 to $2,000. This one
recently sold for . . .
$650

26

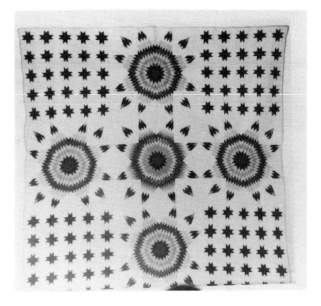

Handmade quilt of unusual
pattern.
$450

Fine Early American appliquéd
quilt.
$1,500

Large zinc hollow-cast eagle with
5-foot wingspan.
$475

27

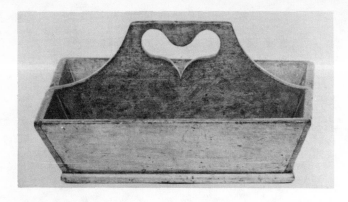

Heart handle drives this painted pine knife box up to . . .
$150

Wooden frame candle mold, with pewter molds. Much better than the only tin ones. Up to . . .
$650

Fire buckets were kept under the stairs with a pillow case and a bed wrench in them—for saving the silver, and the bed if possible. Depending on the scene and condition, up to $1,500. These, each . . .
$350

Ordinary brass bucket from about 1870 with wrought-iron handle, 14 inches across.
$65

Early Pennsylvania pierced-tin pie cupboard.
$425

Small cast-iron coffee grinder in mint condition—20 inches high.
$450

Early American spinning wheel with complete cage for winding yarn.
$275

Country cabinetmaker's idea, more Folk Art than furniture, from a Vermont farmhouse. Around 1870, fit up for granny's convenience on cold winter nights.
$325

Old Farmer's Almanacks were sewn together and bound with cardboard covers and saved. Each . . .
$30

Old Farmers Almanacks, open.

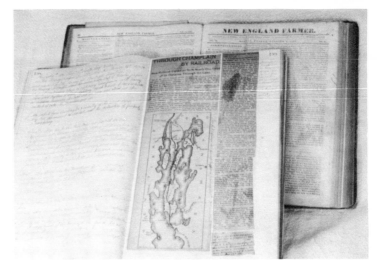

Spyglass used to sight whales by
Captain Ahab.
$225

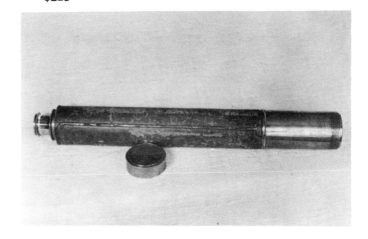

Indian clubs from 1910. The
pair . . .
$30

Stereopticon viewer, **$50**
Cards, **$6** each

Folk Art, painted tin shield, probably done in 1876 in celebration of the respectable revolution.
$450

Painted checkerboard. Folk Art.
$350

Even though the 17-drawer spice chest isn't very old, and was terribly refinished, the demand is great.
$175

Armoires and Wardrobes

French armoire from late 1700s.
One of a pair. For the pair . . .
$1,200

English country wardrobe made of
oak in mid-1800s. Not as highly
valued as French country pieces
for some reason.
$2,000

George III linen press with
flame-mahogany veneer panels.
$3,500

Channel Island armoire. A French kind of piece done to the English taste. Mahogany. Circa 1800.
$3,600

French Provincial armoire from Brittany, after Louis XV style. Early 1700s. Walnut and fruitwood.
$8,500

French Provincial armoire made in the early 1800s. Overdecorated degeneration of the primative Louis XV style.
$3,500

34

An unusual Provincial armoire that may be the missing link between the style of Louis XV and Art Nouveau. Both styles being based on lines found in nature, they seem to meet in this one piece, middle 1800s.
$6,500

Armoire, Dutch, Circassian walnut veneer. Late 1600s.
$2,500

Victorian Spanish-American armoire with the doors removed and fitted with shelves to hold television set, record player, etc.
$175

35

Bedroom Pieces

Plain oak Victorian dresser with marble top.
$300

Pink marble-top Eastlake commode with splashboard. Burl-walnut veneer.
$325

Oak vanity, late Victorian. A Renaissance bouillabaisse.
$325

Late 1800s copy of a Georgian bed with a serpentine canopy. Well-carved mahogany.
$2,500

Walnut Victorian bed. Eastlake.
$350

English carved-oak canopy bed. Centennial, good copy.
$4,500

American Victorian walnut bed of Renaissance style. Fairly simple for such.
$750

Veneered oak bed in turn-of-the-century Fancy Grand Rapids style. Yet to be fully appreciated. But this is an especially bad example, so it commands . . .
$450

French Empire sleigh bed with brass inlay, brass feet in ebony.
$3,000

Chinese opium bed without mattress, circa 1880. Highly carved panels with gold and red lacquer on teakwood. Extra fine condition.
$4,500

38

Country version of a Sheraton canopy-top bed, rope-turned, swelling posts in front, square posts in back. Maple. 1820.
$1,750

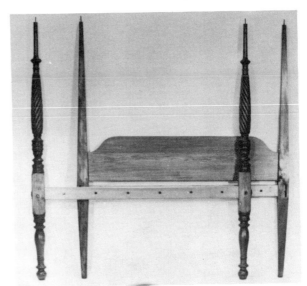

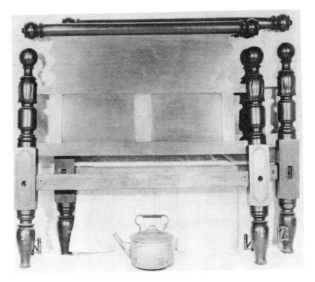

Ball-and-bell four-poster bed, 1870, cherry wood, refinished.
$450

Unusual inlaid Sheraton tester bed with Spanish influence. 1820.
$2,000

Sheraton tester bed without the canopy. Mahogany, 1800.
$1,075

English brass bed with porcelain running up the posts of headboard. Made about 1880.
$1,200

Bed stepladder.
$110

Decorated cottage pine bedroom set. Incredibly undervalued in current market at . . .
$650

Mid-1800s French Victorian bedroom set of ebony on flumed oak. Marble tops. Classic set.
$6,500

Part of stock of beds from 1800–1830. Restored to standard size for modern bedding . . . **$600–$850**

Cannonball and bell bedposts. The most popular design. 1800–1830. Maple. Refinished and widened for modern bedding, $750. "In the rough" like this . . .
   $150

Hired-man's bed showing knobs on frame that were strung with thin rope to support the mattress. Good original red paint. Maple, late 1700s.
   $550

Detail of hired-man's bed. This one is polted from end. Usually they are just pinned, and the ropes hold the bed together.

Benches

A once lovely primitive Spanish hacienda bench with arms that has been desecrated with totally unrelated scrollwork of Empire design in the front board.
$350

Nice primitive old Spanish-influence Mexican bench. About a hundred years old. Not particularly valued.
$125

Six-legged country-made Spanish-influence Mexican bench of the kind that may have suggested calling George Stickley's Morris-inspired furniture by the name "Mission."
$175

42

Bookcases

A Victorian version of George II bookcase on chest. A little bit of everything in design.
$2,500

Oak bookcase with optical glass doors.
$350

Chippendale-style bookcase, circa 1930. Made in England. No such animal in original period. No such glass either.
$850

Grotesque marriage of nice Queen Anne bookcase top to a highboy base with nice Spanish feet, but far too small for the top. But the separate pieces are worth . . .
$3,500

Chippendale bookcase, Centennial reproduction.
$3,500

English Regency bookcase with brass toe-casters. Very rare. Many fakes on the market. This 1840 real one . . .
$1,600

Walnut, glass-doored bookshelf.
$150

How to Buy at an Antique Show

First you have to understand that an antique dealer exhibiting at a show is not some kind of knowledgeable, superior, authoritative person. He or she, or both of them, are lonely, insecure people, far from the emotional supports of their home environment, terrified that they might not even break even on the costs of attending the show.

You have the upper hand. They crave your attention, friendship, and approval for what they are doing even more than they want to make a sale. And God knows they want to make a sale, considering their bill at The Crocodile Motel, the cost of gasoline, a new tire, and so it goes.

So when you spot that incredible sampler you want to buy, at first only look at it out of the corner of your eye or when they aren't watching you. What you want to do is look at everything—and make friends with them. Admire everything. That compliments their taste. Tell them how exciting you think it must be to be in the antiques business. Admire his jacket. Ask her where she got that amazing dress she is wearing. Leave only because you have to meet somebody who you can't wait to bring back to see their wonderful things.

That's the first visit.

On the second visit you're a little calmer, with only a mild gush about this or that. Then you *discover* the sampler. You adore it. But, oh, the price. If only you could afford it. But NO BARGAINING. You shrug a shoulder. Wipe away a tear, and bravely leave their booth to walk down the aisle not looking in any of the other booths.

THEN! The last hour of the show you come to say good-bye to them, and get directions for coming to visit them at their shop. Telling them that you want to bring your "well-off friend whom you couldn't find, but who just *must* see their things."

AND NOW . . . slowly turn for one last look at the sampler.

That's it. If she (or he) doesn't offer to knock down the price of that sampler to what they paid for it, then my name isn't Chicken Little, and the sky *is* falling!

Brass

Brass cannon of indeterminate age, 14 inches long.
$55

Brass cannon—brand new, reproduction. Costs more than an old one.
$80

Reproduction brass spittoon.
$35

Reproduction brass bins for coal or wood at the fireplace.
Left, **$125;** right, **$75**

Brass kettle with wrought-iron handle.
$285

Brass apple-butter bucket without handle.
$65

47

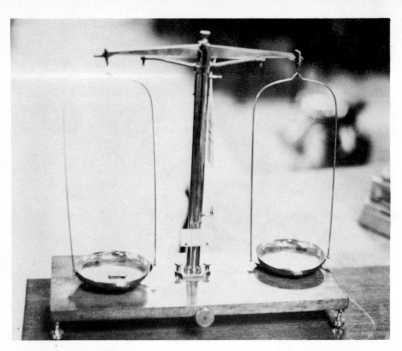

Brass scales for weighing gold
nuggets or arsenic. Apothecary.
English. 1880?
   $275

Russian icon in gilded brass foliage
and black frame.
   $1,250

Breakfronts

Regency breakfront with very little
going for it in terms of proportion.
Still, it is old wood . . .
$4,500

Large breakfront gentleman's
wardrobe with built-in chest of
drawers, m'Lord.
$3,800

Extremely large English breakfront, circa 1800 date established by oval panels. Sheraton. Spectacular piece for spectacular people.
$18,000

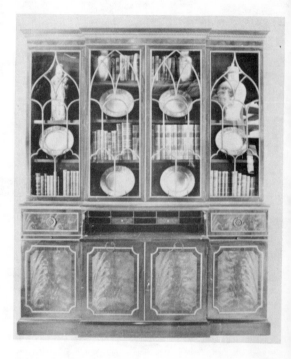

English breakfront, 1820, with center desk drawer or "secretary" added a little later. Sheraton style.
$12,500

Bronzes and Imitations

French-school Art Deco bronze
of early 1900s on black marble
base, 13 inches high.
$2,500

Art Deco bronze figurine mounted
on marble base.
$2,500

Victorian American bronze, 9
inches long of a luxuriously
equipped lady reading a big book.
$1,200

Early 1800s French Empire
clock with bronze classical Greek
woman.
$2,800

Art Deco bronze figure of a girl
mounted on marble.
$2,500

52

French Art Deco bronze with an ivory face, 14 inches high.
$1,250

Big bronze Venus, 30 inches high.
$2,200

Art Deco bronze of girl seated on a bench, only 8 inches high.
$850

53

Bronze figure, 18 inches tall, of a dancing girl with grapes. A *bacchante*.
$1,200

Victorian bronze figurine of Greek Goddess Diana, the huntress, 24 inches high.
$1,000

The Wrestlers, a famous bronze after original Greek sculpture, Italian school, late 1800s, 14 inches high.
$1,800

Bronze of dancing girl, gold patina. French school, late 1800s, 27 inches high.
$2,500

Diana, the huntress and Mercury, 24 inches high. French bronze figures of mid-1800s. For the two pieces . . .
$3,500

On the left, Diana, the huntress, with very smooth patina, 18 inches high, early 1900s. On the right, figure of the French school. Either one, around . . .
$1,500

55

A recasting of Frederic Remington's famous bronze, "Coming Through the Rye." When found, around . . .
$15,000

Bronze horse, made in France, on black, white, and tan marble base.
$1,200

Bronze horse, only 7 inches long.
$800

French-school bronze of
Chanticleer. Late 1800s.
$1,800

Bronze eagle, 16 inches high.
Made in France while Napoleon
was at Elba.
$2,200

Art Nouveau pitcher in white
metal with a fine green glaze over
gold gilt finish that has acquired a
patina. Signed *Jouvant.*
$650

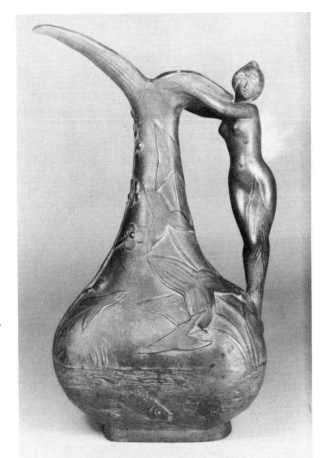

Art Deco cigarette or cigar box in gilded white metal, glass-lined.
$175

Hollow-cast white metal lamp stand from the time that Bobby Jones was king. Washed with a bronze gilt.
$165

Hollow or wash cast white metal (a little stiffer than plain lead) lamp base with gilt wash. Curtain in window space needs replacement.
$125

58

Art Nouveau bronze candelabrum
from French school.
$550

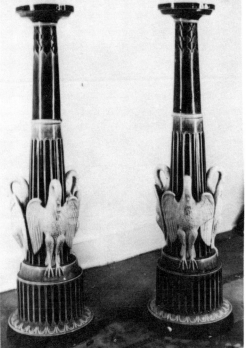

Pair of neo-classical style porcelain
candlesticks with gilded swans,
early 1900s.
$1,800

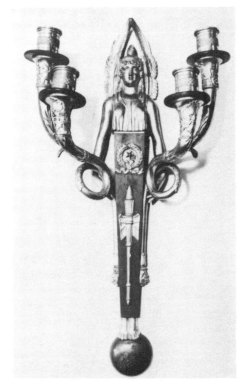

French wall sconce in the First
Empire style; maybe Second.
Bronze.
$850

Chinese gilt-brass, relief-decorated
jardiniere with elephant feet.
Sitting on Moroccan carved table.
Bowl: **$1,500**
Table: **$450**

Fancy Victorian cast-iron mantle
frame, gold-washed. Cupids.
$60

Cabinets-Display

Mahogany curio cabinet of Victorian era in Louis XV style.
$1,200

Victorian carved-oak, curved-glass china case. A crazy . . .
$2,500

Vernis Martin vitrines or curio cabinets made in late 1800s. Style of Louis XV to XVI. However, they are very good and very well made, hard to find in pairs. The pair . . .
$12,000

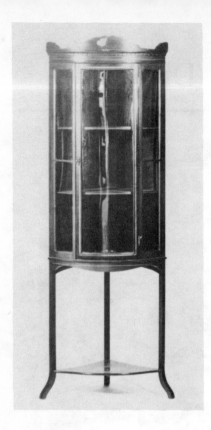

Fancy little curio cabinet. An upright vitrine. Sheraton, made about 1860. Apartment piece Mahogany.
$750

Victorian *étagère* of the 1860s in walnut with gilded figures.
$2,500

Curio cabinet with ormolu decoration around top, fancy brass gallery on top, clover-leaf glass panels. 1850—Regency style. Made in England in the French manner of Louis XV.
$1,850

62

China cabinet made in Chicago circa 1930. Style of Al Capone rococo.
$600

Oak display cabinet used in country stores to display pies. 1900.
$155

Chippendale-design display cabinet. Square legs with spade feet unusual. Pagoda on top. Excellent Centennial.
$2,200

The Secret Place in Canada

Antique dealers are the cagiest people in the world, and wouldn't tell you the time of day unless you bought a clock from them. Which is why it took me almost ten years to find out where the secret place in Canada was. And at that I had to find it out from a picker's helper, who was mad at his boss and drunk to boot.

But he told me true, and when I finally got there a few months later, it was even better than I could have imagined. There was barn after barn full of stuff in the rough, the former contents of hundreds, *thousands* of farmhouses in the eastern townships of the Provence of Quebec. Why? Because the farms had all become too small to operate in the era of big-farm machinery, and a depression had hit the whole area around sixty years ago with bankruptcies and abandonments sweeping the countryside.

On the spring day that I arrived there were eleven trucks lined up at the gate waiting to be loaded one at a time. Which took all day, of course.

If you want to go, take a little Larousse Dictionary, because only French is spoken. Then head out of Montreal toward Quebec City on the new superhighway that runs between the two cities along the southern bank of the north-flowing(!) St. Lawrence river. About three fifths of the way to Quebec City you will see a small white sign that says "DEFOY" and an arrow that points to your right. And about a mile down a gravel road you will start coming on barns stacked three feet high with 100- to 200-year-old chests of drawers, etc., etc. Everything that was in those old farmhouses. And you will be in the secret place in Canada where the antiques come from. Tell the Frères Beaudin that the Furniture Doctor sent you.

CHAIRS

American

Country-made Chippendale chair with slip seat. This one a little low. Stretcher should be about 5 inches from floor. Cupid-bow back. Made of maple, cherry, or mahogany. This one, cherry.
$350

Office chair to use with rolltop desk. Very popular.
$285

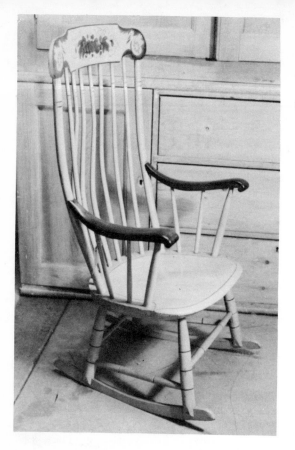

Salem rocker in yellow paint, about 1820s—just before the Boston rockers with roll back to seat. Cherry arms.
$285

Eastlake office chair in walnut. Caster, and leans back on spring. Cane seat restored . . .
$300

Chippendale chair, 1760–80, made in maple, cherry, and mahogany. This one in maple. A country-made chair. As is . . .
$300

Four-slat ladder chair with straight top slat for drying towels. Good condition or new rush seat. Undervalued at . . .
$75

Detail of ladder-back chair.

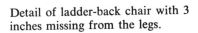

Detail of ladder-back chair with 3 inches missing from the legs.

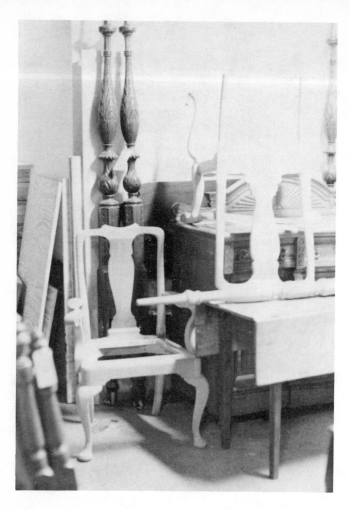

Reproduction Queen Anne armchair at its place of birth in a room behind a big antique shop. All handmade, perfect copy, and quite openly advertised for what it is.
$265

A serious Eastlake armchair in walnut with burl-walnut panels and needlepoint seat and back.
$250

Victorian cast-iron lawn set.
$500

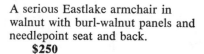

Well-decorated Boston rocker.
$125

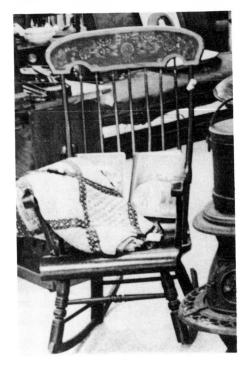

Gentleman's walnut armchair in
grotesque distortion of Louis XV.
$300

Rose-carved Victorian walnut
armchair of the Louis XV
conviction . . .
$25

Walnut, Victorian, Louis XV
armchair. Ponderous and
ostentatious, but . . .
$350

Ornately carved walnut chair with,
at least, Louis XV legs. Maybe the
back is supposed to be Gothic.
$175

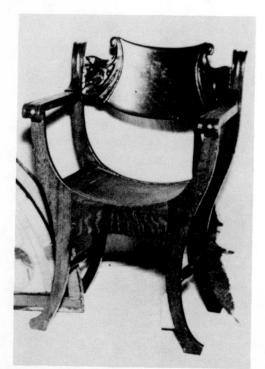

Oak Victorian Savonarola-style
chair.
$225

70

Lady's Louis XV Victorian,
grape-carved chair, still going for
only . . .
$250

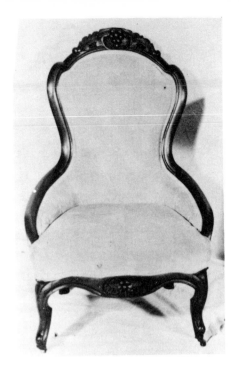

Lady's grape-carved and
finger-molded walnut *fauteuil*-type
chair. Going low at . . .
$350

Ladder-back rocker with Shaker
influence, but with nice little
finials. Maple, splint seat.
$525

Victorian walnut carved chair, a weird blend of Gothic and Louis VI. All strange Victorian pieces still undervalued. Worth three times its current value of . . .
$150

Eastlake walnut armchair with four side chairs, original horsehair upholstery. Still very underpriced on current market at . . .
$400

Gentleman's Victorian armchair with brass ormolu. Louis XV style, circa 1850.
$325

Pressed-back oak Victorian chairs of early 1900s. In sets of four, each . . .
$100

Victorian Eastlake high chair with burl-walnut panel in the splat.
$150

Ladder-back side chair. Common, ordinary garden variety, made all over New England from late 1800s.
$40–$70

Bannister-back side chair. Good turnings on legs, but a weak crest rail. Original button feet are good. 1770. Currently about . . .
$275

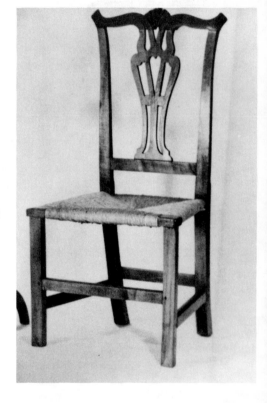

Well-proportioned Early-American country Chippendale, very overlooked for a long time. Invest in them like you should have in IBM. Look for carving on the crest rail. Dates from around 1790. Still going for peanuts at . . .
$150–$175

Country Chippendale side chair with a slip seat. Fine boldness of legs and back. Usually found in cherry, sometimes mahogany. 1790. Quite underpriced, but going generally for . . .
$250

74

Belter chairs of laminated rosewood, circa 1860, made in New York City. The best pieces bring much higher, but these are about, for the pair . . .
$16,000

Pair of Belter chairs of laminated rosewood. Not the best. The pair . . .
$8,500

Country Chippendale side chair with a little Victorian paint on it. 1790, and very underpriced at current . . .
$150

Highly carved American Victorian furniture is an outstanding riser in value. These sets are hand-carved, unusually unique, come in long sets—up to ten or twelve in a set. They average an amazing, per chair . . .
   $700

Empire side chair with a fiddleback in that always desirable, curly maple, cane seat, made circa 1875. Real sleepers as they are still going for only around . . .
      $125

Country-made chair reflecting the Empire style that the French brought to Mexico under Napoleon's nephew and his Empress Carlotta. Parallels our country-made English chairs.
      $135

Totally scraped Victorian chair
with an English back and Empire
influence in arms and legs.
$125

Modern reproduction of a
Mexican's idea of a Louis XV
fauteuil chair . . .
$165

English

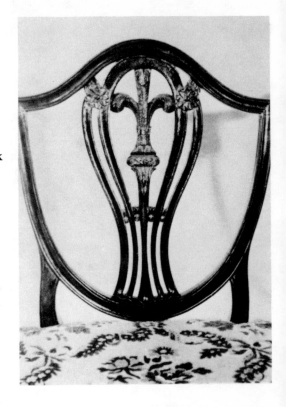

Period Hepplewhite shield-back side chair with fine carving.
$850

Oak reproduction of an early English gaming chair.
$250

Queen Anne side chair with inlaid marquetry. A Centennial, made in England around 1876.
$500

Pair of Victorian-made armchairs in imitation of the Carolean period. Made in England. The pair . . .
$1,500

Queen Anne side chair imported from England. Acanthus-leaf carving makes it transitional to Chippendale (George I). Strong pad feet and good carved knees, but probably Centennial. And not in a set.
$350

Country Queen Anne side chair with Spanish (from William and Mary). Good turnings and stretchers, but back is flat instead of curved. 1760. However, relatively early and rare in U.S.
$1,000–$1,200

Chippendale ribbon-back chair with slip seat. About 1800. Not really sought after and underpriced at current market value of . . .
$250

Regency armchair, commonly called Sheraton in the U.S. Made about 1860. Not very popular, so available for as little as . . .
$100–$125

Country Chippendale chair with a slip-in rush seat. Nice ribbon back. Made about 1820. Legs are short, but not cut off, so probably used as a slipper chair in a bedroom.
$400

Hepplewhite side chair with nicely carved back and spade feet. Urn back is transitional toward the Sheraton period.
$500

Set of George I chairs with unusual round shield-top backs in the usual mahogany, slip seats. Set of eight: two arm and six side chairs. Good Centennials.
$5,500

81

Very dull, style-free set of eight
Edwardian-Victorian reproduction
chairs. Even so, the set . . .
$3,000

English set of eight ladder-back
chairs with straight Chippendale
legs. In mahogany. Centennial
reproductions. The set . . .
$4,500

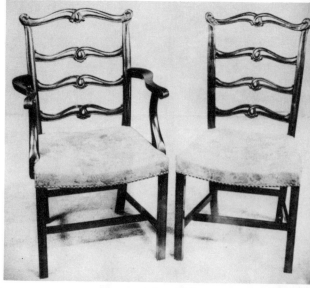

Extremely elaborate Victorian
version of a Chippendale armchair.
Ribbon back and bird-head arms.
Strange paw over ball feet.
Mahogany. For those with
eclectic taste.
$1,600

82

George I chair with pad feet, sunburst carving on top rail. Walnut piece of the period.
$2,200

Side and armchairs from a set of eight Edwardian reproduction of the Queen Anne style. Weird devil heads on front rail. Hoof feet. Fine lines. Set of eight . . .
$8,000

Ribbon-back Chippendale-style side chairs made in late 1800s in England—i.e., Victorian reproductions. Centennials. The pair . . .
$1,500

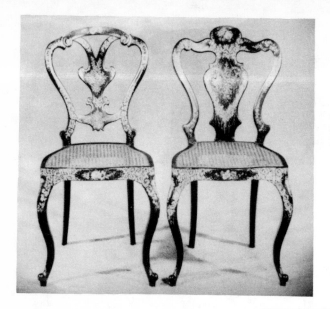

English Victorian papier-mâché
side chairs. Mother-of-pearl inlay
and painted flowers. Cane seats.
Each . . .
    $525

Edwardian-period Queen
Anne-style chairs, burl-walnut
backs, shell-carved knee, pad foot.
The pair . . .
    $1,500

George III (Chippendale)
armchair. Actually of the period.
    $2,200

84

Pair of armchairs showing oriental influence, with marble plaques in backs from mid-1800s. Teak with mother-of-pearl inlay. For the pair . . .
$3,200

Pair of Queen Anne into George I armchairs with cloven-hoof feet and eagle-head arm ends. Gilt highlights on walnut. Very good Centennial copies of the late 1800s. Pair . . .
$3,000

Chippendale or George III corner chair made out of oak. Centennial.
$850

Chinese-style red-lacquered chair.
To look like carved cinnibar.
Folding chair.
   $1,800

Pair of highly carved teakwood
armchairs made in late 1800s. The
pair . . .
   $3,500

Fancy

Arrow-back chairs with step down on the crest ridge, strong rabbit ears, bamboo turned legs. 1810. Matched set of six chairs, **$250 each.**

Step-down back Windsors, made in 1800. The pair . . .
    $400

Simple Windsor chair with yoke-back crest. 1810. Pine seat, maple turnings.
    $110

Bird-cage Windsor. Back too large
for chair, so only worth . . .
$150

Bird-cage Windsor rocker with
short arms, original rockers. 1810.
Currently underpriced at
around . . .
$300

Stick-back Windsor rocker,
original rockers, set-back arms to
accommodate hoop skirts. Early
1800s.
$325

88

Fancy Sheraton settee from
around 1840. Bamboo turnings.
$300 up

Step-down back Windsor settee,
fair paint, double-chair base, and
even though legs have lost about 3
inches in leveling them off, a piece
like this goes currently for . . .
$2,500

Excellent Mammy Rocker with
nice back and good roll to the
arms. Original tender pulls out.
Long rockers in back to prevent
tipping over. 1820.
$500

Settee on rockers, early second coat of paint, about 1820, seat like a Salem rocker.
$1,200

Thumb-back side chairs with short spindles. Quite late—1850, on verge of mass-production—such as Hitchcocks. Set of five for only . . .
$450

Set of five chairs made by somebody who also made Boston Rockers. With decoration in good condition . . .
$650

Fancy Sheraton chairs that
Hitchcock mass-produced, 1820.
Restored and refinished, the five
chairs . . .
        $1,200

Fancy Sheraton side chair, cane
seat, about 1860, and very
collectible when in curly maple as
this one is. In sets of six or eight
they run about $275 a piece. But
for a lone single . . .
        $250

Hitchcock chair, circa 1840. Pillow
back and original decoration
—from Sheraton design. In the
rough, only . . .
        $75

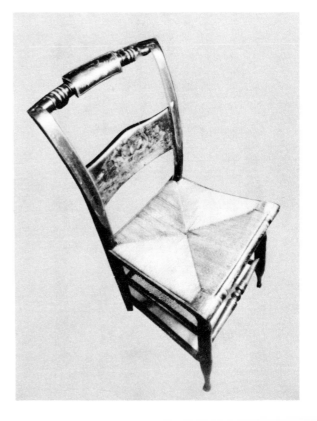

91

Turned

Slat-back armchair with mushroom arms, good proportions. 1750.
$850

Turned armchair with replaced feet and new grips at ends of arms. Carver influence on back. About 1740. Even with repairs worth about . . .
$800

Bannister-back armchair in curly maple, but arms don't match the rest of the chair. High crest is good. Around 1870.
$750

Country bannister-back armchair of about 1770. Poor proportions.
$850

Early ladder-back chair with a cute little bar across the top for hanging a towel. About 1760. Rush seat.
$250

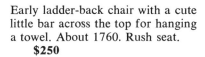

Hoop-skirt rocker, slat back, maple turnings nice and fat. Made about 1800.
$250

Portuguese side chair with rush seats and nice paint job. 1760. Off the auction block in London $700. In the U.S., only . . .
$200

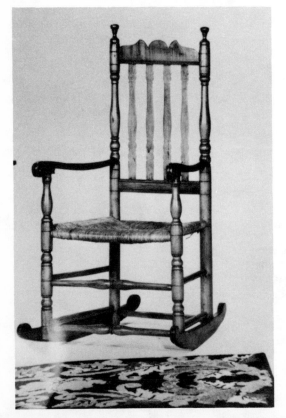

Maple bannister-back with good crest and interesting rockers added later. Dates 1790.
$400

Buyer beware is the name of this bannister-back armchair. Very suspicious flat arms, heart carved in the crest is almost too good to be true. If "right" $2,500. This one . . .
$650

Country Queen Anne with decent paint on it. Made about 1760. Fine proportions.
$1,000

Shaker rocker with towel bar on top. Known as a "Number Seven" after the factory in Mt. Lebanon, New York, where they were made. So many of them around that they go for as low as . . .
$450

Upholstered

Martha Washington armchair of the Hepplewhite period, 1810 in U.S. Widely reproduced by cabinetmakers, and sold for around $850. This original one . . .
$1,200

Martha Washington chair transitional from Chippendale to Hepplewhite. Poor square back, but genuine if confused.
$1,200

Queen Anne wing chair of nice proportions. But restored feet keep price down to . . .
$1,500

Chippendale wing chair. Nice bold curves to the wings done by excellent upholsterer. 1790. All original legs.
$2,500

Very fine Irish Chippendale wing chair with superb carving on legs and apron that goes all around. Ball-and-claw feet on front, Queen Anne on back. High, broad back.
$2,500

Chippendale open-armed lolling chair on coasters to reestablish length of legs that were clipped off to level it.
$1,100

Hepplewhite sofa that looks like a box. 1810.
$1,000

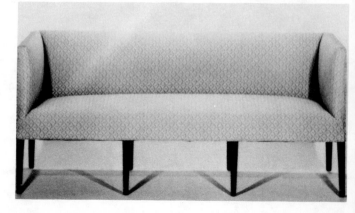

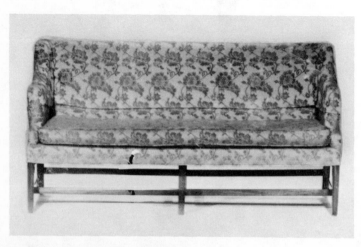

Country version of Hepplewhite sofa, fat arms, but good stretcher base. 1810.
$2,000

Fancy Sheraton with sort-of
Angelica Kauffman decoration on
three-panel cane back. Cushion
over cane seat.
$550

Chippendale window bench. Of the
period.
$1,400

Pair of wing chairs in the William
and Mary style, newly
reupholstered. Victorian-made
Centennials. 1890. The pair . . .
$2,200

99

French two-part chaise longue in style of Louis XV, covered in needlepoint, which is important to its value. Walnut, made in France 1890. (French Centennial.)
$2,500

Walnut Centennial upholstered armchairs, often called board-of-directors chairs. George I, Queen Anne into Chippendale. Each . . .
$700

Heavyweight Victorian version of a Chippendale chair with grotesque masks in carving. Walnut.
$850

100

Pair of *bergère* chairs from the
Louis XV period, gold-leafed. The
pair . . .
   $3,500

Pair of authentic French Empire
chairs.
       $3,500

Pair of chairs of first period of the
French Empire. The pair . . .
       $3,500

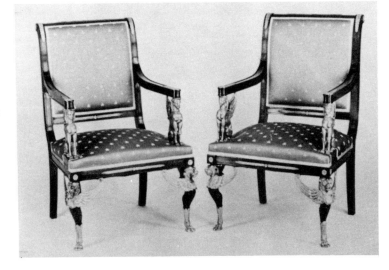

Pair of Victorian Renaissance armchairs.
$750

Gainsborough chair made in Victorian era. Basic Chippendale with hysterical extra carving.
$850

Wing chair with block-and-turn stretcher, Queen Anne legs, 1710–50, crewel fabric. It's a perfect copy—individual made by a good cabinetmaker, as is a common practice. Real one: $5,000. This one . . .
$850

102

Reproduction English Queen Anne
wing chairs done in leather just
like the real thing. Each . . .
$1,400

Pair of carved armchairs from
Hong Kong, late 1800s. Each . . .
$800

Windsor

Comb-back Windsor rocker from about 1800.
$550

Crazy country Windsor rocker with wild comb and corner knobs on top of back. The kind Folk Art people go for. No paint. 1800.
$600

Very rare form—a bow-back Windsor settee about 3½ feet in length. In fine condition, made about 1800. And get ready . . .
$4,500

Fine comb-back Windsor armchair with bold turnings, flaring top. 1790.
$1,500

Comb-back Windsor armchair with weak arms and even weaker turnings. Even so, because it is a real comb back made around 1800 . . .
$1,000

Bow-back Windsor armchair with pedestrian turnings all around. 1800.
$650

English-origin Windsor armchair of oak. Typical thin seat and typical back. Worth twice as much in London as here. Here . . .
$150

Bow-back Windsor with fine
continuous arms, strong turnings.
1790.
$2,400

Two bow-back Windsor side
chairs, one on the right has
interesting brace back, making it
worth $100 more than the one on
the left, which is worth . . .
$550

Windsor writing armchair of nice
proportions with two early coats of
paint. Made 1780.
$2,500

Bow-back Windsor with the bamboo leg, 1790–1810. The more spindles in the back, the better, and this has the most valuable nine. Maple legs in pine seat.
$325

Thumb-back kitchen Windsor chair about 1830. Pine seat, the rest maple, or birch or ash. Oak top splat on this one.
$85

Bow-back Windsor chair, refinished, all original, but not much style to it. So only . . .
$300

Windsor chair of the mid-1700s
with big round seat. The best are
$1,500, but this one is only . . .
$800

Child's potty chair, seat hole filled
in. 1820.
$135

Chests of Drawers

Nice Chippendale bureau with five graduated drawers, curly maple—the magic word.
$3,500

Chippendale block-front bureau. U.S. Front is blocked in a full 2 inches, good drop in the apron, molded edge top. If no parts replaced and with original brasses . . .
$15,000 and up!

Chippendale 4-drawer bureau in maple. Replaced base frame is too big. If all original, this country piece would be worth $1,500. But with replacement base . . .
$550

Four-drawer Chippendale bureau with nice graduation in drawer height, nicely shaped top, on ogee bracket base. 1780.
$3,000 and up

Country Hepplewhite bow-front bureau, mahogany box with bird's-eye maple drawer fronts. Strong apron, but rather rough workmanship.
$900-$1,100

111

Hepplewhite bureau, weak top and flare of French foot. Replacement brasses.
$1,200

William and Mary bureau with 2 drawers over 3. Replaced ball feet, burl-walnut-veneered drawer fronts, nice molding around drawers. With original feet around $5,000. This one . . .
$2,000

English oak, ball-foot chest. Dates from circa 1720. Good carving, paneled end, tear-drop pulls original. Pieces like this rising fast over last two years. Currently worth around . . .
$2,500

112

Country-made Sheraton bureau.
Almost into the Empire period as
top drawer extends over the
bottom 3. Painted grain on front.
A $100 bureau with $400 worth of
paint on it.
    $500

Sheraton bureau with straight
front, reverse graduation of
drawers, coming close to Empire
period. Proportions uninteresting,
so only . . .
    $425

Sheraton bow-front bureau with a
deck top, pretty good rope carving
coming down corners with
pineapples on top of it. Probably
made around Salem,
Massachusetts, and terribly
underpriced at this point.
Mahogany crotch veneer. 1820–40.
    $600

A country version of a Sheraton bureau in great bird's-eye maple, with fine delicate legs. Drop on apron was an inspiration—keeps it from looking like a box. Graduated drawers. And like all such country-made pieces, undervalued.
$650

Sheraton bureau, 1820, mahogany-veneer drawer fronts, curly-maple posts, birch sides. Weak top. Made 1820–40. A country piece.
$625

Hepplewhite bureau from around 1800. Fine proportions, good heart shape in apron, good flare to the French feet. Lots of line inlay in mahogany veneer. Very popular established style.
$2,000 plus

114

Hepplewhite chest with nice
scalloped apron.
$1,200

Mahogany Hepplewhite swell-front
bureau, missing 2 inches from the
feet, so only . . .
$1,200

Grain paint on 4-drawer
country-made bureau in
Hepplewhite manner. Weak top,
poor leg and apron shaping, but
tall legs are good. A $200 bureau
with $400 worth of original paint
on it.
$600

Square, chunky Hepplewhite bureau with decent workmanship and from early 1800s, but still a dog. And since aesthetics still count for something, you should be able to buy it for . . .
$650

Cherry ox-bow-front bureau that falls right after the block-front period. Strong graduation, but top too small. Made about 1780. Solid mahogany.
$5,500

Ball-foot, 4-drawer chest, grain paint. 1740. Very sought after.
$4,000–$6,000

Strong Hepplewhite with nice flare to base, graduated drawers. Made around 1800.
$1,800

European bureau—French? Italian? Strong market. Auctioned in U.S. for $400–$500—going for $2,500 plus in London. 1780. Current U.S. price . . .
$600

Walnut bachelor's chest with flip-out top. Late 1700s. Basic Georgian design. Very popular, even with lots of restoration . . .
$2,500

117

Unusually nice Georgian chest
with 12 drawers, bracket feet,
flame mahogany. Hard to find a
12-drawer chest.
$3,500

Curly-maple Queen Anne chest
from New England. 1770.
$5,500

Tall chest with peacock carving
instead of fan. Cherry. 1760–80.
From New Hampshire. Actually
the top of a highboy resting on
new frame.
$2,600

Country Queen Anne chest on frame with fine center drawer with fan carving, grain-painted very dark. 1770.
$1,250

Fine Queen Anne chest on frame, big bold feet. From New Hampshire, much like those made by the famous Dulap family. 1780. In maple. A country-made bureau worth an easy . . .
$10,000

Queen Anne block-front chest of drawers with bun feet, thought up in south Germany. Chinoiserie lacquered front. Made in late 1800s.
$2,500

Marble-topped Eastlake dresser.
$600

Early Empire chest of drawers
with matched African
crotch-mahogany-veneered front.
A "sleeper" on the market, they
say, but I've heard that for the last
thirty-five years.
$350

George III serpentine chest with
original pulls, splay feet.
$2,300

Craftsman's chest, set on a new
base. Early 1900s. Great coffee
table, so . . .
$350

North German dower chest from
early 1600s. Trumpet feet. In U.S.
only . . .
$1,800

Military chest in sections with
flush brass handles for easy
packing on ships. Legs unscrew
and go into drawers for transit.
Super footlocker. Made in Orient
for British officer.
$1,600

Military chest made in Hong Kong for the British officers. Camphor wood. Brass flush handles.
$1,600

Military chest made of camphor wood on turned bun feet that unscrew to fit in drawers for tight packing.
$1,500

Unusual blanket chest with a hinged top and 2 false-drawer fronts. English, oak, ogee bracket feet. Late 1700s.
$2,000

Heavily inlaid Persian chest. 1870, and about . . .
$2,200

Persian chest heavily brass inlaid. Made about 1770, found in England.
$1,200

Oak icebox. Small one, brass fittings.
$350

123

Highly collectible miniature chests,
old English and Victorian. From
left to right . . .
$650 and **$250**

Miniature chest in pine with ball
feet and tear-drop pulls of the
William and Mary influence. Made
somewhere in Europe at some date
or other (?).
$200

Chests—Lift Top

Hepplewhite country chest with strong apron. Lift top for storing blankets. A $300 pine blanket chest with $550 worth of paint.
$850

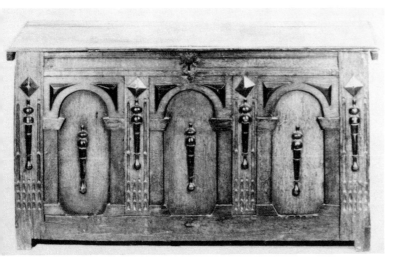

Called American "Pilgrim Century" with split-spindle decoration. Often really English in origin. (Called Jacobean in England.) Hard to tell the difference. If English, only $1,200. If can be proven American . . .
$4,500

A little ditty box, possibly used aboard ship. Heavy baille handle on top. Two keyholes.
$125

Classic pine 6-board blanket chest with fine half-circle legs. Early one—1780. Nice molding around base.
$250

Small 1-drawer blanket box. Very popular. Some old red paint on it. 1760.
$400

Conventional country 6-board pine blanket chest made 1810. Worth about $225—with $1,000 worth of paint and decoration on it.
$1,225

126

Only 18-inch-long ditty box, much sought after. Without paint $175, with paint . . .
$250

Traditional 2-drawer blanket chest. Refinished, so pine grain is showing. Hepplewhite style, country made. Refinishing has cut its value by two thirds.
$250

Six-board chest from around 1850, original paint.
$150

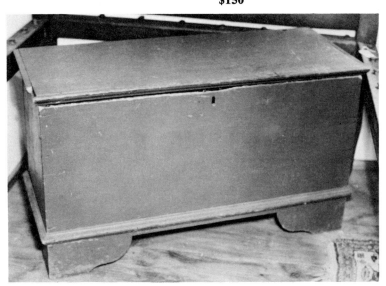

Six-board blanket chest with
bootjack end which makes it
early—1790–1810. Sticks under
the ends of the lift top make it the
earliest kind.
  $285

Chest on newly made frame.
Candlewood.
  $385

Small decorated dome-top trunk.
Sometimes found covered with
deer hide. Always the wrought-iron
handles at the ends. Pine.
  $250

William and Mary oak coffer with raised panels.
$1,400

Ball-foot blanket chest—the best. Back legs come right down from the side board. Only 2 bottom drawers are real, top lifts. In red paint with original hardware. Pine. 1750.
$6,500–$7,000

Old Spanish chest made in Mexico circa 1850. Wrought-iron fittings. Recent carving inflicted on the front board to supposedly make it more interesting. *Chacun a son goût!* Louis XV "suns"?
$375

129

Chest-on-Chests

English Chippendale
chest-on-chest. Architectural top
with heavy quarter-columns,
smallish bracket base. 1790. Fine
hardware on figured mahogany.
$4,250

American maple chest-on-chest, 5
drawers over 4, good drawer
graduation. 1790. A country-made
piece.
$4,500

Oriental chest covered with engraved brass. Trade-ship period—1870. Korean out of Hong Kong harbor. Full of small drawers.
$6,000

An interesting tall bureau that is all one piece, originally built into the wall of a house, so back boards are replacement. From Connecticut. Chippendale, heavy wood. 1800.
$6,000

English chest-on-chest.
$3,200

English chest-on-chest.
$2,500

English chest-on-chest.
$3,700

132

On Running Out of Antiques

Yes, Virginia, they are still shipping us antiques from England. And by the container-load. Probably about three or four a week. And all a big dealer or wholesaler needs to do is pick up his telephone and say, "Send me one of them $7,000 containers!" Or a $15,000 one. Or $20,000 one. And he can specify early or late Victorian, or heavy on the Hepplewhite—and get what he pays for.

Since as far back in the 1920s the gloomsayers were already predicting that the antiques would "run out," where does it all come from—and the flow even increase?

The answer is that even as far back as 1776 there were sixty-five million people in Great Britain. Given an average of only four pieces of furniture owned by each of them, that's 260 million pieces of the eighteenth-century stuff. Then in the almost one hundred years of the Victorian era, another 400 million pieces must have been manufactured. So, far from running out of antiques—the best is yet to come!

Clocks

Terry pillar-and-scroll clock with some restoration, but all original including reverse painting on glass.
$1,500

Pillar-and-scroll shelf clock of the Terry style. With any maker's label inside will bring from $1,250 to . . .
$2,000

134

English bracket clock, about 1760, nice ormolu decoration. In London $4,500. In U.S. . . .
$2,500

Made in late 1800s, but this bracket clock has complicated movement that plays Westminster chimes, or runs silently. Brass door mountings.
$2,500

Pressed-oak gingerbread clock. Currently going for a ridiculous . . .
$275

135

Gingerbread clock from late 1800s, missing it's top. ($275 with top.)
$150

Carriage clock with repeating button on front of top for finding out the time in the dark. Good porcelain face. 1820.
$1,800

American clock with a brass dial, flared French feet. Not attributable to any maker, so only . . .
$1,200

Shelf clock with dial flaked off of Empire period. For the handy man.
$85

French shelf clock with ormolu decoration.
$650

French Empire bracket clock with brass figures.
$8,000

French Crystal Palace marble bracket clock with brass lion.
$3,500

Calendar clock, tells day of month on bottom dial.
$450

Simulated marble clock, dried-out pine and light as a feather. If it was a real marble one—$300. This wooden one . . .
$135

138

Empire shelf clock with rosewood veneer. 1840.
$275

Regulator clock used in offices and schools around turn of the century.
$275

Simple copy of an English bracket clock—now just a mantle clock. Made around 1900. Good works and sound.
$175

Miniature steeple clock, mahogany veneer on pine. Even with some chipping of veneer . . .
$225

Regulator clock in oak. 1910.
$350

German 2-weight regulator clocks. Beware of imitations, which are rampant. These real ones from 1850–90 are each worth around . . .
$1,500

Banjo clock with some flaking of face, but original reverse-painted glass. No maker's name.
$650

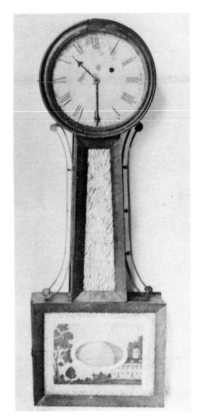

Conventional banjo clock. Even with replaced glass in the throat . . .
$900

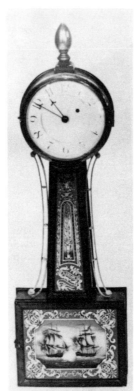

An "A. Willard" banjo clock, mahogany, original glasses.
$1,750

Daniel Pratt & Sons regulator
clock in oak case.
$650

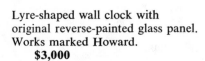

Lyre-shaped wall clock with
original reverse-painted glass panel.
Works marked Howard.
$3,000

Satinwood balloon clock made
about 1800. Brass feet, classical
painted decoration.
$700

142

Wooden painted jeweler's trade sign from Maine.
$400

Sèvres clock set about 24-inches high.
$16,000

Clocks—Tall

Scotch grandfather clock in oak.
$850

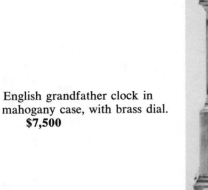

English grandfather clock in
mahogany case, with brass dial.
$7,500

Georgian, tall case clock with
chased brass face and swan-neck
pediment. Burl-walnut front
surfaces.
$3,000

144

English grandfather clock of late 1800s with painted face and mahogany case.
$4,500

Brass-faced Georgian English tall case clock with disappointing flat top (original). Mahogany case.
$2,000

English grandfather clock. 1790.
$7,500

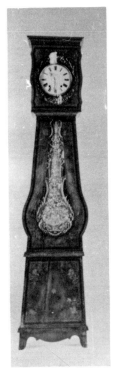

Country French grandfather clock. Originally a large wag-on-the-wall, which has been mounted on a base. 1790.
$6,000

145

Tall case clock with unusual top.
Country cabinetmaker product.
Wooden movement run by weights.
1800 copy of 1760 style.
   $2,000

Tall case clock made around 1900.
Brass dial, rolling planets. Fancy
system of chimes pushes its value
up as high as . . .
   $3,000

English grandfather clock in highly
carved oak case, with brass dial.
$6,500

Tall case clock made in late 1800s.
But has Westminster tubular
chimes inside, elaborate movement.
Case highly carved in Chippendale
manner, 3 brass finials over broken
arch. Brass face—everything!
   $7,000

Carved oak from around 1905, lots
of chimes, and for some
worth . . :
$3,000

Chippendale clock case in curly
maple.
$4,500

Walnut grandfather's clock with a
wooden dial face from early 1800s.
One-day (30-hour) movement.
New 8-day brass movement with
chimes have been put into this one.
$1,200

Commodes

Commode from the shop of the
French cabinetmaker Linke.
Marble top and exuberant gilded
bronze decoration. Kingwood.
Exercise on the Louis XV theme.
Made in late 1800s.
$25,000

Georgian commode. There's an
opening to support Granny's potty
behind the false drawers. Usually
remodeled by putting in real
drawers. As is . . .
$650

Provincial Louis XV marquetry
inlaid commode, late 1700s.
$2,600

French Empire commode made
in late 1800s in the tradition of
those made in early 1800s.
$1,500

French commode with ormolu
and Sèvres plaques. Late 1800s.
$2,500

149

Adam-style corner cupboards made in U.S. around 1900. Marble tops. Custom-made (as opposed to factory-made). The pair . . .
$1,300

French-made server or sideboard with marble top, chinoiserie panel on doors. Made around 1930.
$850

About "Centennials"

A "Centennial" is a piece of furniture that looks exactly like an authentic piece of Queen Anne or Chippendale. Even the finish looks old and worn, and the wood underneath has deoxidized enough to acquire a patina. But the trouble is that while it *is* old, it is only barely 100 years old, instead of 200 years plus, like authentic Queen Anne and Chippendale. And there is a lot of it around.

The story behind it is that during the late 1800s in Victorian England the English discovered their past, and these two styles were revived by the furniture makers of England who now had steam-powered machinery and could mass-produce. But the mass-production applied only to the roughing out. The final surfacing and finishing were still done by hand. And this finish work was minutely faithful to the design and hand carving of the original pieces.

The result, of course, is a reproduction, but an almost perfect *and already old* reproduction. And undoubtedly, on certain occasions they have been passed off for the real thing. However such deceit has practically disappeared with the recent recognition of the value of these pieces for what they are.

In fact, today it is not unusual for an interior decorator to pay four to $5,000 for a really good Centennial dining table and set of eight chairs. Bringing the retail price to . . . well, supposedly plus 20 percent for a reasonable profit. Which isn't bad when you consider that furniture stores standardly mark their goods up 40 percent! *Antiques are always your better buy.*

Couches, etc.

Centennial copy of a settee with eagle arms, heavy claw-and-ball feet, lovely back. As is . . .
$1,800

French Empire chaise longue.
$1,600

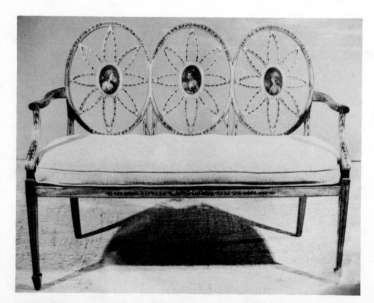

Typical triple-back settee in Hepplewhite-Adams style. Definitely Adam decoration. Hand-painted portraits in backs. Cane seat. But a copy made circa 1880, in England. Hard to find.
$2,500

American rosewood rococo revival
Victorian chaise longue, circa
1860. Fruit carving.
$1,600

Empire style chaise longue made in
Holland with marquetry inlay.
$1,500

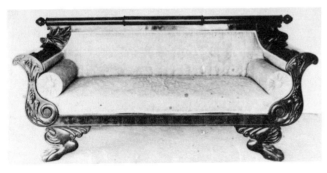

Federal Empire mahogany sofa
with rather coarse carving. Very
late, commercial.
$600

Reproduction of an American
Early Empire couch also called
Federal. But this is of Victorian
era, so only . . .
$1,400

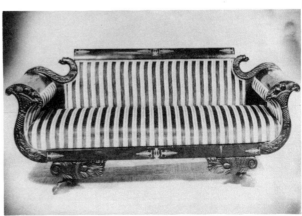

Laminated rosewood Belter parlor set. The real thing.
$42,000

Walnut-carved sofa in the manner of Belter.
$1,200

Medallion-back Victorian expression of Louis XV style that is about as fine as they come. Sits lightly, almost floats like the real thing. Way underpriced on today's market at . . .
$650

Medallion-back love seat in the Victorian Louis XV style.
$350

154

Walnut Victorian finger molding love seat in imitation of Louis XV.
$500

Finest kind of grape-carved, finger-molded, medallion-backed Victorian sofa in Louis XV style.
$650

The rolling curves Empire as they were simplified in the U.S. in early Victorian era. But the extra coiling in the back is the Mexican version.
$650

Unusual entrance-hall French settee. Painted white and antique glazed. Louis XV style. Centennial, of course, and a hard piece to sell because it's hard to find a place to put it.
$1,500

Victorian sofa with Empire influence.
$250

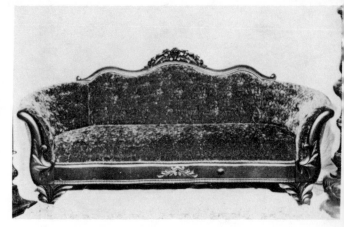

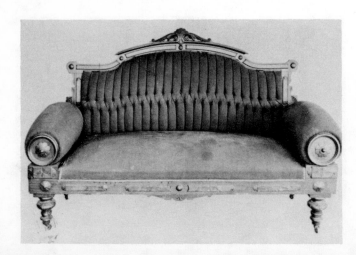

Walnut Eastlake sofa with strange cushion arms from the Turkish fad.
$400

Queen Anne settee with
shepherd-crook arm. Centennial
reproduction.
$2,200

Mahogany Hepplewhite
shield-back settee. A Centennial
piece.
$1,100

Three pieces of matching English
furniture in the Gothic-
Chippendale style. Made in
late 1800s. Rare to be both Gothic
and a set.
$3,500

Fancy-carved mahogany couch
with inlaid back and front under
Spanish influence.
$800

157

Reproduction of Louis XV sofa
made around 1900.
$2,500

Sheraton custom-built sofa with
nice carving. Made circa 1945.
$750

Sheraton sofa with eight delicate
legs (better than six). Nice reeded
arms. Made about 1810.
$2,500

Camel-back Chippendale settee. A
Centennial reproduction.
$1,350

Art Nouveau upholstered settee in
fruitwood with a lovely lady in the
middle. In need of a little
restoration of the finish. Recently
stolen at a big auction in New
York City for only . . .
$2,400

Victorian-made Carolean-style
settee.
$1,100

Carved teak settee from Hong
Kong.
   $1,700

Burmese carved *tête-à-tête* chair
made mid-1800s.
   $3,500

Cradles

Early Canadien-style cradle in pine, brought down from Quebec.
$250

Finely chip-carved cradle with Scandinavian influence in design.
$700

Hepplewhite spade-foot swing cradle in mahogany—some repairs.
$750

Primitive country-made pine cradles. Hooded on the left; scalloped on right.
Left **$325**
Right **$175**

Cupboards

Pine corner cupboard with nice open top, probably from Pennsylvania. Nicely refinished. 1820.
$1,450

Two-part corner cupboard with glass door and well-shaped apron. Pine, made about 1820.
$1,700

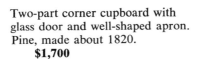

Super little corner cupboard.
Looks older, but made around
1810. Pine.
$1,500

One-piece corner cupboard with a
little architectural design running
up the sides and across the top of
it. Cloverleaf shelves. 1820.
$2,000

Corner cupboard originally
plastered into a house. Nice solid
plank door. Pine. A real simple
beauty before some creep scalloped
the sides and fronts of the shelves.
Late 1700s, so still selling to
culture-free persons for . . .
$1,800

164

Pine corner cupboard made around 1820. One of America's finest original designs before being destroyed by the Visigoth who scalloped those side boards. Original H-hinges. Bought by people who hate good design for . . .
$1,200

Pine corner cupboard in robin-egg-blue paint.
$1,800

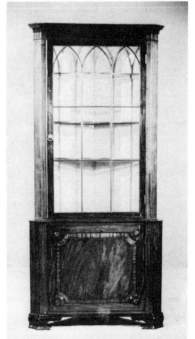

Mid-Georgian corner cupboard with Gothic arches.
$3,500

English oak corner cabinet of the
(more or less) Queen Anne period.
$7,500

Jacobean-style English Victorian
reproduction of a
bookshelf-cupboard. In oak.
$1,800

French Provincial buffet *à deux
corps* (two bodies). Made of
French pine in late 1700s.
$4,500

166

Classic pine country cupboard from circa 1850. The scalloping is an atrocity committed by a cretin probably in the 1920s. How could anybody even *think* of doing such a thing? Even so . . .
$1,200

Fine French Provincial cupboard with blind doors at the top. Late 1800s.
$8,500

Pine kitchen cupboard from late 1800s. Restored and refinished for dining room use.
$1,050

Simple cupboard with nice paneled doors, made around 1770. Simple board shelf interior.
$4,000

Three-foot high "Parson's Cupboard" that rested on a table or stand. Pine; could have been made almost any time. But a fast seller.
$175

The most sought-after of cupboards. Pine, board door in the bottom. Often reproduced. Real Early American look of late 1700s.
$2,800

Usually from Pennsylvania or Ohio, these pieced, tin-paneled pie safes were popular in the late 1800s. Run $400–$800. This one . . .
$550

A clothes press (or dresser in England). Pre-Victorian, pine, refinished. Sort of Empire-looking. Very useful, so . . .
$1,800

Hardware store cupboard with original brass handles and plates to hold identification cards. Pine. 1900.
$1,000

Victorian rose wood *étagère*, made in U.S., but French Empire inspired.
$1,600

Unusual whatnot because it has cupboard on bottom. Walnut. 1880. Renaissance style.
$425

Decoys

Average garden-variety duck decoy. This one from Maine. Really old, or recently made and distressed—either way . . .
$35

Pair of snipe shore birds worth about . . .
$85

Duck decoy with nice carving on bill and around the eyes; lead weight still on the bottom. Goes for around . . .
$85

171

Carved wooden goose decoy of no particular age.
$100

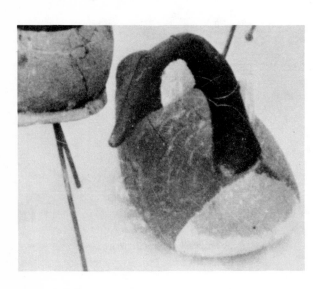

Carved wooden goose decoy of no particular age, but bent neck.
$125

Carved wooden duck decoy with nice detail in wings.
$100

Pintail decoys. Each . . .
$85

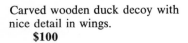

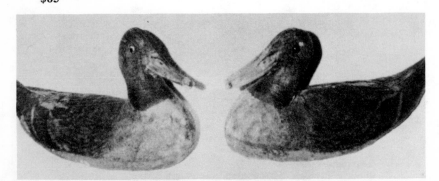

172

Maine decoy with in-leaded head.
$150

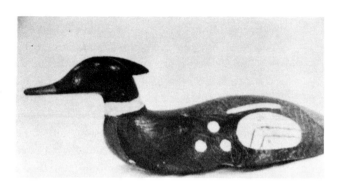

Nova Scotia decoy.
$175

Carved Canadian geese on spikes,
originally from Prince Edward
Island. Each . . .
$100

Primitive duck decoy.
$100

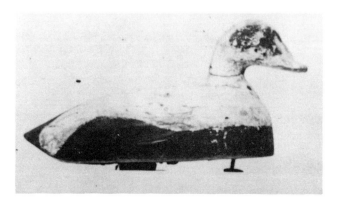

173

The Great "Georgian" Nonsense

The most common use of one-upmanship in the whole antiques business is the use of the term "Georgian" to describe a piece of eighteenth-century English furniture, because since there were three King Georges during that century, that leaves you to figure out if the piece is Queen Anne, Chippendale, a blend of those two, or Adam, Hepplewhite, or Sheraton. Or some blend among two of them.

The way it works out among the more plain-spoken people in the interior decoration business is as follows:

George I refers to the transitional pieces between Queen Anne and Chippendale, when more and more carved decoration "in the French Manner" (as Chippendale himself called it) was being added to the basic Queen Anne lines.

George II refers to the fully realized Chippendale style. Meaning, of course, the basic Queen Anne lines richly decorated with rococo carving. A small aesthetic achievement, to be sure, but nevertheless currently still the most popular of the eighteenth-century designs since antique furniture has always been mostly bought by people with more money than taste.

George III refers to English furniture styles of the Greek Revival that swept Europe following the discovery of the ruins of ancient Pompeii. That is, Adam, Hepplewhite, and Sheraton.

Desks

English mid-1800s partner's desk. Mahogany, leather top. Strong rise in value lately.
$4,500

Chippendale partners' desk, which has the same drawers on the other side, of course. Nice mahogany, but a Centennial reproduction made about 1880. However, still . . .
$4,000

Plantation desk, made about 1830–50. With podium. Cherry with leather insert—Empire style.
$165

175

Desk on frame commonly found
painted, from late 1700s. Some are
tavern tables with desk boxes put
on top. But this one is authentic
in maple and pine.
$2,500

Wooten desk, made in U.S. at
height of Eastlake Victorian
period. As this is a comparatively
small one, only . . .
$15,000

Hepplewhite tambour (sliding
reed-paneled doors). Lid falls down
over drawer. Mahogany drawer.
These are currently undervalued
at . . .
$1,400

Very rare Chippendale (with strong Empire influence) architect's desk that expands as shown in accompanying photo.
$12,000

Architect's desk, expanded.

Architect's desk from behind.

177

Hepplewhite tambour desk with inlaid legs. A Centennial reproduction.
$1,500

Counting-house desk with gallery on top to keep papers from falling off. Five graduated drawers. Nice old pine, simple Shaker look—but not. Early 1800s, but real "Early American" look.
$1,400

Louis XV style marble-top lady's desk. Centennial copy.
$1,500

178

Made in America about 1900, an idea of a French desk—sort of Louis XVI.
$1,200

French Second Empire ebony *bonheur du jour* or lady's writing desk with brass fittings and mother-of-pearl inlay. As all ebony is undervalued . . .
$1,200

Eighteenth-century European kneehole desk, bracket base.
$1,250

179

Bureau du plat in ebony with ormolu (gilded bronze) decoration. French Centennial reproduction.
$3,500

Lap desk mounted on new stand to match it triples the value. Walnut.
$425

Trade-ship goods from Hong Kong. China trade, 1870. Carved teakwood desk with marble inserts. Made to please. Legs are Chippendale, Queen Anne, and Louis XV all at the same time. Intricate carving.
$1,800

180

Desks—Barrel-Top

English lady's barrel-top desk. Writing surface slides out, has tooled leather on it. Hepplewhite. **$750**

Closed view of lady's barrel-top desk.

Cylinder top desk with chinoiserie decoration from Victorian England **$1,200**

Renaissance Revival Victorian cylinder desk of mahogany and walnut.
$1,600

Unusual double desk with rolltop on both sides. Made around 1800 in Austria. Figured mahogany veneer.
$6,500

Oak Victorian S-shaped rolltop desk that has been, for some unknown reason, wedded to a Spanish table made some thirty years earlier.
$275

Early 1900s oak rolltop desk.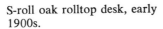
$600

S-roll oak rolltop desk, early 1900s.
$1,500

183

Tambour-top table desk. Top goes all around. Hepplewhite or George II, as you prefer.
$1,500

Tambour front, 1830, William IV desk. (That's English version of French Empire.) Rope-carved legs typical of the period. Beautifully designed piece. Perfect proportions.
$3,500

American rolltop desk circa 1880. Walnut and walnut veneer. S-roll. Gallery top, paneled sides. Top of the line—walnut a lot more desirable than oak.
$5,200

184

Desks—Slant Front

Curly maple is the magic word, and this relatively narrow desk is a popular size. Reproduction brasses. Base is old, but not of same wood. Even so, it will sell—being curly maple—for . . .
$3,000

Badly mangled Chippendale desk. The base is a replacement and looks it from afar. Crude fan carved in the door at a later date. Made 1830. But you are buying a fast look, and the look is worth . . .
$1,200

Chippendale desk with a nice-looking interior, interestingly shaped base, original wooden knobs in this case. From New Hampshire. 1780.
$2,500

Chippendale desk with ball-and-claw feet. From about 1780. Gentle ox-bow front, original brasses.
$3,500

Nice 1790 Chippendale desk with upside down interior for no good reason. (Stuff slides out of cubbyholes.) But nice mahogany grain.
$2,500

Chippendale desk in maple that sold at auction in 1964 for $350. All authentic. Today's price, the usual . . .
$2,500

Chippendale desk in heavily grained birch. Only three drawers, which makes it a little bit lower for writing.
$3,200

Ordinary maple Chippendale desk, all authentic. All of them worth at least . . .
$2,500

Serpentine-front desk with
Chippendale legs and Hepplewhite
pulls, made about 1880—a
Centennial piece.
$1,200

English Empire, painted—note
black paint flaking off of gessoed
columns at side. Blocky Empire
legs are too pushy. Nevertheless,
should bring . . .
$1,100

Early desk with Queen Anne
bracket on base, made around
1760. Maple, painted dark red.
Even with some restoration . . .
$3,700

188

Queen Anne desk on a frame made about 1760 in maple (legs), pine (across the front), and birch (inside). Very poorly carved fan certainly done much later. It's simply out of place. Cuts value down to . . .
$2,000

Super Queen Anne desk. Curly maple, the super wood. Dates 1740. Legs pin up into the base like William and Mary ball feet—old! Found in Concord, New Hampshire, farmhouse. Recently sold for . . .
$11,000

Circa 1900 reproduction small lady's desks. The one on the right is pretty good Queen Anne style. The one on the left is chop suey of Spanish feet, William and Mary, Queen Anne, Chippendale. Either one . . .
$1,000

189

Simple Golden Oak Victorian
thin-against-the-wall desk made
about 1910. No applied carving on
front, so only . . .
$175

Nice example of cloven pony-foot
with hair hanging over it,
exaggerated acanthus-leaf carving
on knee. It's a desk-on-frame
Centennial pipe dream. Curiosity
value . . .
$1,000

Lady's desk of the Golden Oak
Victorian period. The typical boxy,
office-furniture look, except it sits
on those delicate French legs.
Amazing.
$175

Simple little country desk, nailed together in around 1810. No class, and fair proportions are an accident. But has "Folk Art" charm with box on top.
$250

Marquetry-inlaid bureau-desk, bombe-shaped. A copy of a Dutch piece, this one was made around 1890. Brass gallery should be removed.
$2,200

Two-lid writing desk with beaded legs and front in pine that is typical of the primitive Spanish furniture in Mexico. Circa 1850, pre-Victorian.
$225

191

Burl-elm slant-top desk. Authentic
Georgian. Because of the unusual
wood, 1750.
$4,500

Oriental carved teakwood from
1870–90 clipper-ship China
Trade. Out of Hong Kong, where
it was made for export.
$2,500

So-Called "Instant Refinishing"

A trick known to most antique dealers is that a dirty old shellac finish can easily be wiped off with rags dipped in a bowl containing either denatured alcohol or lacquer thinner. The old shellac simply dissolves on contact with either of these fluids. And neither of them will raise the grain of the wood or blemish the surface in any way.

Furthermore, since the pores of the wood still remain sealed with shellac after the "washing" off of the old surface finish, all you have to do to create a new finish is to wipe the piece with a thin coat of boiled linseed oil or tung oil, and let dry for a week.

And how can you tell if the finish on your piece is shellac? That's easy, because all furniture was finished with shellac up to the era of Victorian oak, when modern varnishes came into use. So if your Hepplewhite sideboard was refinished in the last eighty years, someone may have put a "modern" varnish on it. In that case . . . no instant refinishing.

Earthenware

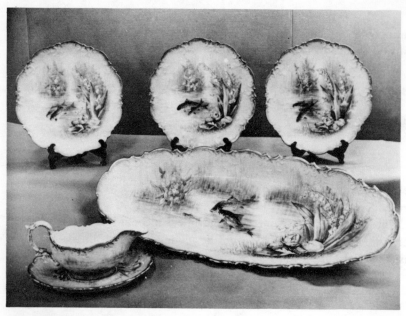

Late 1800s Limoges fish set.
$600

Fine old china cup.
$12

Limoges cup and saucer.
$18

Tea set.
$150

Royal Vienna tea set, maroon,
signed panels.
$1,200

Tea set with oriental motif.
$150

Ironstone soup tureen with cover,
in perfect condition.
$65

Rose medallion tureen complete with top and underliner. Good handles. Depending on size . . . **$650** and up

Capo di Monte tureen on stand from late 1800s.
$1,200

Nanking covered tureen for serving chop suey, of course. Large size . . .
$800

196

Wedgwood bisque biscuit barrel.
$150

English Victorian pottery pitcher.
$250

Pitcher without bowl.
$45

Pitcher and bowl of late 1800s.
$150

Octagonal-shaped English platter
of mid-1800s, blue and white.
$150

Rose medallion porcelain basket of
mid-1800s.
$750

Latticework basket with an underliner. Butterfly pattern of rose medallion. Perfect condition . . .
$600

Real rose medallion punch bowl. Mandarin figures. Trade-ship period—1860 and up.
$1,500

Rose medallion punch bowl, this one often called butterfly medallion. Made for our China trade-ship period—the 1860s. Condition is the main thing with these bowls. This one is perfect.
$1,200

Butterfly medallion punch bowl. 1880 China-trade product. Very desirable design.
$1,250

Two pieces of mocha ware. On the left a seaweed decorated mug. On the right a large decorated mug with checkered design on top.
Left **$125**
Right **$225**

Rose medallion shaped tray from a fitted condiment set. 1860.
$500

Canton China wash basin missing its pitcher.
$800

Japanese Imari punch bowl made in 1890. Large, vivid colors.
$1,850

200

Imari of fine quality, featuring mandarin figures. A chop plate. 1890 China-trade china.
$600

Chop plate of Imari from 1920s period in more muted colors than the earlier plates of 1890.
$350

Staffordshire china platter with a Delaware State coat of arms on it. Made in England, blue.
$900

Chinese flow-blue plate.
$30

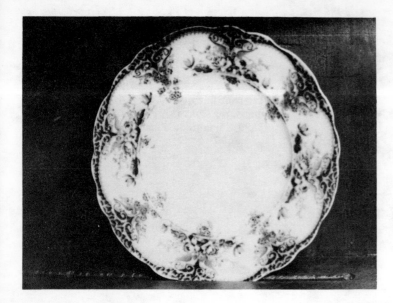

Flow-blue platter.
$30

Flow-blue platter.
$125

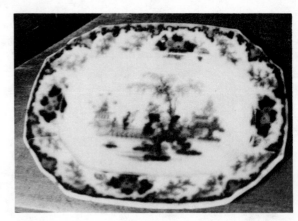

Colorful dishes, each . . .
$3

Fireplace Items

Wrought-iron andirons in blade design with little brass finials. Date around 1780. Made by good blacksmith.
$850

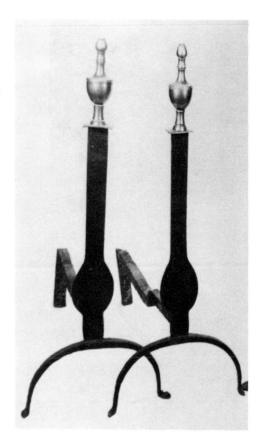

Wrought-iron andirons made about 1780. Goose neck, diamond head, trace of penny feet.
$300

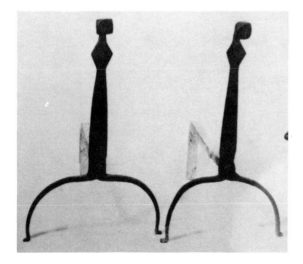

Ordinary goose-neck andirons with penny feet and blades. 1780.
$300

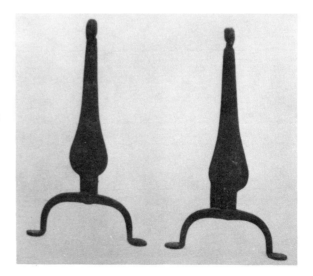

Chippendale brass andirons.
$500

Conventional pair of brass
lemon-top andirons with snake
feet, made about 1800.
$550

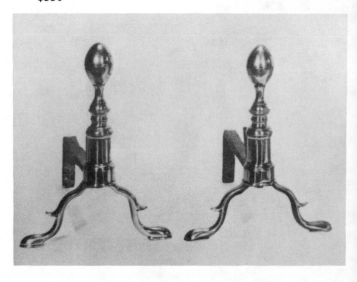

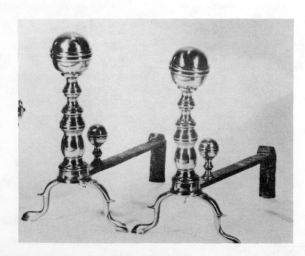

Pair of brass 1800 andirons,
Boston type.
$275

Brass bed-warmer with simple
handle and engraved lid. Currently
up to around . . .
   $200

Fake wrought-iron trivet with
revolving top for turning dishes
nearer to the fire as it sits in front
of the fireplace. Still, they sell to
some people for . . .
   $400

Glass

Pair of Sandwich glass candlesticks.
$150

Two Tiffany iridescent favril glass goblets and a small vase.
Goblets, **$200** each; vase, **$350**

Pressed-glass pitcher from late 1800s.
$35

Typical English pressed-glass cruet set. Salt, pepper, vinegar, mustard, etc.
$65

Cut-glass cruet set, pewter tops, enamel decoration, silver plate.
$175

Victorian pressed-glass compote.
$35

207

Gold-rimmed, etched crystal,
extensive service set. A piece . . .
   $20

Bohemian glass ruby-flashed
decanter, cordials, and liner plate.
$275

Tantelus or decanter set in a case.
Or liqueur set. Etched glass.
Walnut-and-ebony case with
mother-of-pearl and brass inlays.
Late 1800s.
   $1,600

208

A group of early kerosene and whale-oil lamps in pressed or pattern glass. The whale oil lamps are from the 1700s up to around 1850, and run from **$75** to **$200**. The early kerosense lamps, from **$50** to **$125**

Glass paperweight inkwell with pewter cap.
$75

Diamond-cut glass inkwell.
$65

Decanter set with boulle work—complicated brass inlay in satin and rosewood.
$1,400

209

Two blown bottles. The pair . . .
$125

Dark green bottle.
$85

Eiffel tower bottle originally
containing the French version of
Za-Rex syrup for flavoring kids'
drinks.
$25

210

Pair of leaded-glass windows, 24
inches across.
$150

Leaded-glass window, 3 feet high.
$250

211

The New Antiques: Mission

As the years and times of life go by everything gets a little bit older, even as you and I. And the latest style of furniture being flacked for admission to the antiques club is the misnamed Mission furniture first manufactured by George Stickley in Syracuse, New York. (And some dealers jump up and down if a piece is found with the label intact.) But it still looks like an orange crate that was made by a German cabinetmaker who apprenticed in a tank factory—heavy slabs of oak, bolted squarely together.

Mission raises the question of whether anything that gets old enough is of value. And what is the difference between fashion and style? Well, Mission is certainly getting older and dealers who can still buy it very cheaply are working hard to make it fashionable. But style—and charm and grace—it will never have.

So my secret friend and I have left it out of this price guide lest we encourage the flimflammers who are hawking it at puffed-up prices.

Hall Pieces

Oak hall tree with mirror and box seat.
$350

Walnut Victorian umbrella stand.
$275

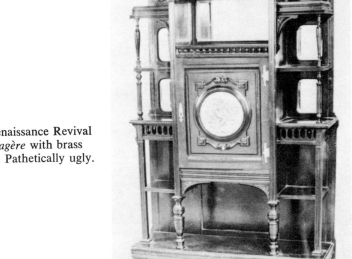

American Renaissance Revival mahogony *étagère* with brass center shield. Pathetically ugly.
$1,000

Eastlake Victorian hall piece with
long mirror.
$800

Victorian hall piece in walnut and
white marble. Renaissance style.
$1,500

Highboys

Typical example of an English fitted cabinet on stand. William and Mary, circa 1690. The real thing.
$8,500

Queen Anne highboy in oak from the early 1700s, but a really ugly duckling, so only . . .
$3,500

Conventional Queen Anne highboy with delicate legs. Nice fan on apron is special. All original. 1760.
$8,500

Simple country highboy of late 1700s with good Queen Anne legs. However, the pieces are "married"—the top being plainer than the bottom with it's fine fans. But still . . .
$3,750

Highboy base waiting for a happy marriage. Nice Queen Anne legs and fan. Maple. Circa 1730. Crazy price rise in the last two years just as I predicted. From $650 then to current . . .
$1,650

Queen Anne highboy base—not a lowboy. It's heading for a marriage to some top, so now is worth around . . .
$1,500

216

Queen Anne-married highboy with glass knobs replacing the brasses in Victorian era.
$1,800

New Hampshire highboy with an architectural top, Chippendale ball-and-claw feet. 1780. Cherry, original finish, and perfect condition . . .
$18,000

Undistinguished Queen Anne highboy of about 1780. Fan carving and concave center drawer in base. 1780.
$4,500

Indian Items

Old Indian headdress with turkey feathers and beadwork across front. Plains Indians, circa 1880.
$350

Southwest Indian vase-shaped basket about 10 inches high.
$200

Engraved tomahawk peace pipe from Plains Indian tribe.
$400

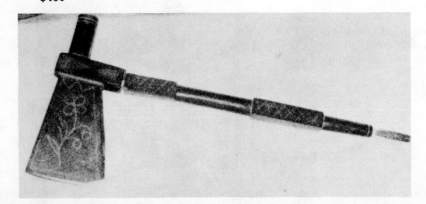

Copies of cigar-store Indians. Hand carved and painted. Average price . . .
$650

Southwest Indian bowl-shaped basket 18 inches in diameter, circa 1800.
$250

Southwestern Indian baskets. From left to right: vase-shaped, $850; bowl-shaped, $25; vase-shaped on far right with human figures, $750. The tall basket with animal figures and cover top is Eskimo.
$900

219

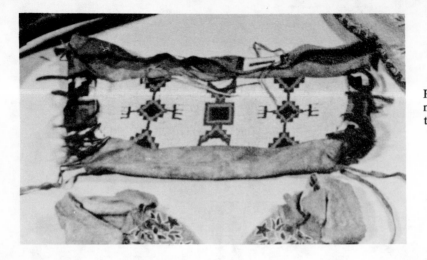

Plains Indian (Sioux?) beaded necessaries bag, 20 inches across the front, circa 1880.
$500

Beaded pipe bag of Plains Indians, circa 1880.
$300

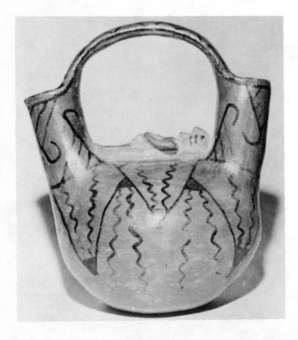

Indian wedding jug from the Southwest.
$125

Lighting Fixtures

Fancy Victorian hanging parlor lamp with hand-painted shade and font and cut-crystal prisms, brass frame.
$500

Cast-iron hanging Victorian parlor lamp with decorated glass shade.
$350

Cloisonné floor lamp of Victorian
Turkish period, 1875–1900.
$800

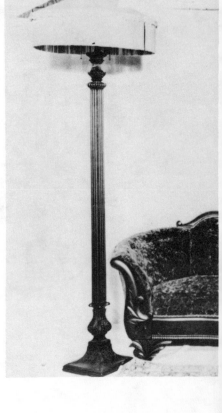

Mahogany floor lamp circa 1915.
Silk shade with tassels and fringe.
$175

Victorian lamp with fancy white
metal base with replacement ball
shade ($25).
$185

Slag-glass-panel lamp with bronze base.
$250

Typical nickel-coated brass kerosene lamp. Electrified.
$95

Electrified nickel on brass kerosene lamp made in late 1800s. Replacement shade costs $15.
$125

Fancy lamp, embossed, new
shade in case glass—green outside,
white inside. Electrified.
$125

Electrified brass lamp with
cranberry-glass shade.
$95

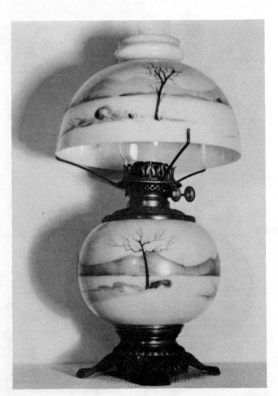

Decorated lamp with original
painted shade.
$235

On this lamp white tam-o'-shanter shade has replaced original ball top that was painted like the base.
$150

Marble-based kerosene lamp with a glass-etched font. Sheraton influence—early 1800s, with new parchment shade. Electrified.
$175

Pin-up lamp with bracket (for hanging on a nail) for wall or walking service.
$65

Victorian wall-bracket kerosene lamps. Cast iron, glass, and brass. The pair . . .
$110

Hanging light used in offices and country stores. All tin.
$125

Hanging brass country-store kerosene lamp.
$175

Pair of kerosene lamps. The pair . . .
$125

Simple glass finger lamp for going up the stairs to bed.
$45

Milk-glass-based kerosene lamp.
$85

Deitz railroad lamp designed for
swinging, red glass. As is . . .
$45

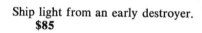

Ship light from an early destroyer.
$85

Farm lantern with good broad
base for safety in the barn. Heavy
glass lense.
$85

228

Port and starboard lamps about 8
inches high with original kerosene
lamps still inside. The pair . . .
$35

Pair of brass port and starboard
lights about 18 inches high.
$525

Electrified coach lamps, the
pair . . .
$350

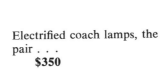

The "Other" Auction Houses

Everybody knows about the famous auction houses in New York City. Christie's, Sotheby Parke-Bernet (rhymes with *stark Bernadette*), Phillip's, and the William Doyle Gallery. They get all the publicity, because they serve the international community and get the record-breaking prices for the very best from the very rich.

But there is a second layer of auction houses spread around the country catering to good, active dealers and interior decorators. These houses hold auctions on a regular basis, and anyone can attend and bid. After you pay five or ten dollars for the "admittance catalogue." And they all allow you to inspect the merchandise the day before the auction.

Here are some of the best of these houses. In case one of them is in your area, you can drop them a line, and they will let you know about upcoming auctions. Auctioneers are all friendly people. Civilized, too.

Garth's Auctions, Inc., 2690 Stratford Road, Delaware, Ohio 43015

The Wilson Galleries, Verona, Virginia 24437

Morton's Auction Exchange, 643 Magazine Street, New Orleans, Louisiana 70190

Julia's Auction Barn, Fairfield, Maine 04937

Richard W. Withington, Inc., Hillsboro, New Hampshire 03244

C. G. Sloan & Co., Inc., 713 13th Street, N.W., Washington, D.C. 20005

Bonner's Barn, Malone, New York 12953

Robert C. Eldred, Inc., East Dennis, Massachusetts 02641

Clements Antiques of Texas, Inc., Forney, Texas 75126

Clements Antiques of Tennessee, Inc., 7022 Dayton Pike, Chattanooga, Tennessee 37343

Douglas Galleries, Route 5, South Deerfield, Massachusetts 01373

F. O. Bailey Co., Inc., 137 Middle Street, Portland, Maine 04111

Milwaukee Auction Galleries, 4747 W. Bradley Road, Milwaukee, Wisconsin 53223

Knight's Antiques, 4750 East National Road, Springfield, Ohio 45505

Military Items

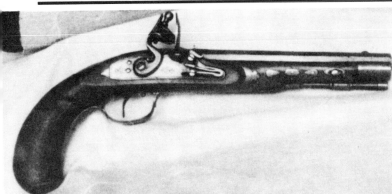

Rare inlaid and engraved
Kentucky flintlock pistol.
$2,500

Civil War officer's swords.
Depending on how
interesting they look . . .
$200–$500

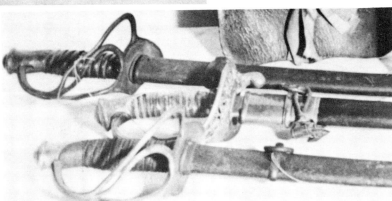

Civil War officer's epaulettes in
carrying case.
$550

Presentation Civil War
sword with insignia.
$1,100

Mirrors

Good Queen Anne mirror of 1760
with painted top, 18 inches high.
$1,500

Adam-style mirror (not Bilbao)
with urns, original glass.
$950

Cushion-molding frame mirror of the Queen Anne period in U.S. Grain painted, exceedingly rare.
$2,400

Courting mirror with reverse painting on glass in the frame.
$650

Shaving mirror from early 1700s. English—Georgian. Gilt decoration around mirror.
$1,500

233

Centennial reproductions of English, Queen Anneish shaving mirrors. Either one . . .
$300

Tortoiseshell frame mirror, early 1700s. Notice the two pieces of original glass.
$1,300

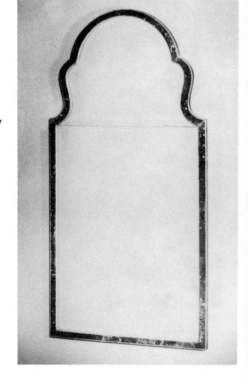

George II style good architectural mirror frame. Gilded. Circa 1740. Broken-arch pediment with a central cartouche.
$1,800

234

Late Victorian vanity mirror made of tin.
$55

Ogee mirror of Empire period with mahogany veneer soaked off to reveal the "Early American" pine under it.
$125

Mirror with gilded cast-iron frame with holders for candles. Victorian. One of a pair. The pair . . .
$185

235

Empire frame of mahogany veneer on pine, containing print of no particular value.
$40

Ornate Victorian (French Rococo) mantel mirror.
$100

Miscellaneous

Globe on stand, circa 1915.
$250

Brass telescope on tripod, late
1800s, with small sighter-scope,
caps, and case.
$1,400

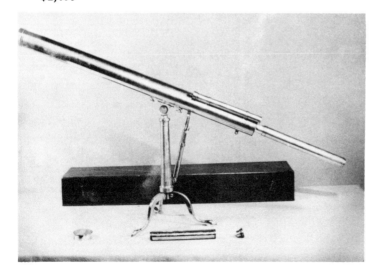

Eastlake dental cabinet with marble top and burl-walnut veneer
$2,500

Walnut dental cabinet with roll-down front, marble surface. Late 1800s, English Victorian blend of styles. Almost Eastlake.
$2,500

Mahogany dental cabinet of Victorian origin.
$550

Oriental dressing table with matching stool. Decorated lacquer.
$750

238

Victorian fitted sewing table in very fancy walnut veneers and carving. Paw feet.
$800

Pole screen of papier-mâché with mother-of-pearl inlay. English Victorian. Empire-curved legs. To keep the fireplace light out of your eyes while playing chess.
$350

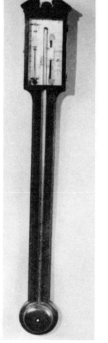

Georgian stick barometer, circa 1780.
$850

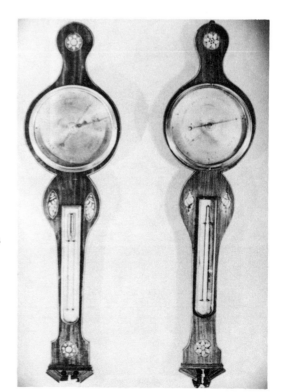

Victorian-made English barometers with brass faces. Each . . .
$850

English folio or map holder.
Victorian-made. Walnut.
$1,400

Popular table that turns into
library steps. Made in England in
1875. Current reproductions only a
few hundred dollars, but this one,
believe it or not . . .`.
$2,200

Bamboo magazine rack.
$75

Cast-iron dictionary table,
adjustable height, walnut top.
Victorian.
$135

Oak file cabinets go with rolltop
desks, so these go for . . .
$250

Very colorful seed catalogue used
to show farmers what they would
get when they bought seed from
traveling salesmen. Sixty
hand-tinted prints.
$600

Hand-sculpted marble figure about 4 feet high, made in Italy circa 1875.
$3,500

Parisian vanity-table decorative head from the 1920s.
Hand-painted plaster of Paris.
$15

Parian lady with a jug.
It's a casting made with ground-up marble. Don't wash it! It dissolves.
$125

Plaster of Paris cast of Venus de Milo from Victorian art school.
$32

Reproduction French telephone.
$65

Regina upright disc music box,
together with fifty discs. Victorian.
$6,000

Victorian oak fireplace mantel.
$350

Oak chairs.
$125 and **$200**

Brass-and-mahogany Victorian plant stand.
$225

Victorian copy of a Queen Anne smoking stand. Or rather a smoking stand in the Queen Anne style. Mahogany.
$250

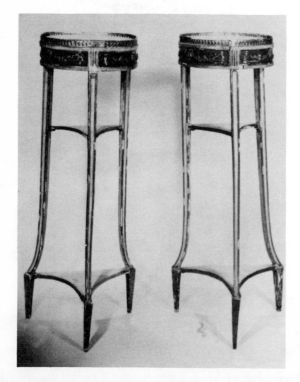

Good pair of English lamp stands with brass galleries on tops. Three legs for stability. Sort of French Hepplewhite. The pair . . .
$1,200

Early American baby-tender in pine and maple. 1840. Not sought after.
$140

English bird-cage on a Sheraton frame. Very sought after in England, and worth over $2,500 there. In the U.S. . . .
$1,200

Pennsylvania dough box made about 1820. Breadboard-type top. Maple and pine.
$450

Porcelain plates, transfer-painted, early 1900s. Each . . .
$150

English lavabo for washing your hands, of course. Water tank on top, basin below. Taken from a wall and mounted on a French Provincial frame made for it. Pewter. 1780.
$2,200

Rosewood music box with built-in clock, plays twenty tunes. Made in Europe, 1850.
$2,500

Fresian-carved wood foot-warmer. Probably Swedish, vividly painted. A tin pot with short legs fitted inside of it to hold hot coals.
$275

Lacquered chest from China with pewter insert, a tea box made for the clipper-ship trade period.
$250

Imported from Holland. No comment.
$250

Gout stool. Reproduction.
$450

Tortoiseshell boxes. Tea caddy on
left, 1830. On right, jewelry case.
Tortoiseshell can no longer be
imported into U.S. Either box . . .
$750

Georgian cellarette on later stand.
Brass binding.
$1,700

William IV cellarette with winged
feet. 1840.
$1,200

Iron kettle to go with the iron
kitchen stoves.
$65

Copper kettle. Victorian.
$85

Continental Georgian-style silver
tea set made in 1800.
$1,000

Large ornate, silver-plated tea and
coffee set.
$350

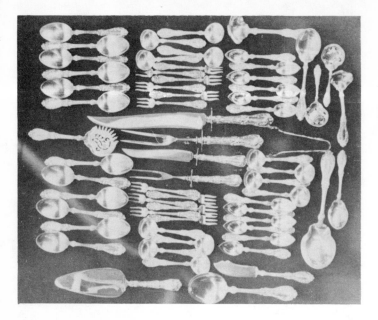

Sterling silver with fancy handles. Finest quality, but not old. Each piece . . . average . . .
$60

Set of silver-plated dining instruments. Run of the mill.
$350

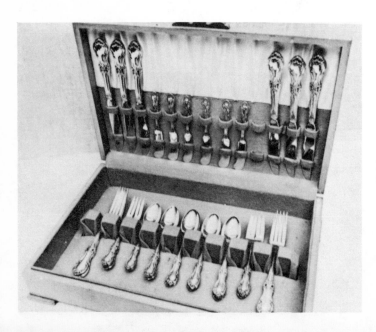

Sterling-silver flatware service. Depending on age, weight, and maker, these range from . . .
$1,000–$10,000

250

Spanish traveling trunk with wrought-iron fittings mounted on new frame for storage without stooping.
$150

Old cast-iron balancing scale with brass plates that don't fit. But Spaniards love them.
$65

A really nice bench about a hundred and ten years old in its natural patio environment.
$450

Ornately carved Mexican bar. Old wood used for frame. Carved panels are new and a good expression of Mexico's current exuberance about life. Destined for a stockbroker's apartment.
$950

Detail of carving on Mexican bar.

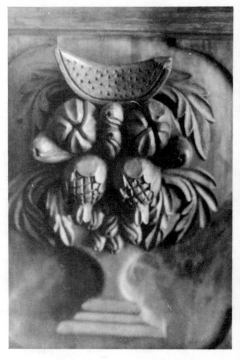

Eight-foot-high doors from an old hacienda in Mexico. Originally straightforward Spanish lines have been ruined with recent decorative carving by some moron interior decorator.
$450

252

Ox cart from Great-Grandaddy's hacienda. More atmosphere in your patio-garden.
$350

Old wagon wheel for propping up against the wall of your garden or patio. A drag on the market.
$45

Pancho Villa's saddle is here mounted on a pedestal made from an old architectural turning. It is absolutely the real thing, and there are about 150,000 of them for sale in Mexico. But it does add atmosphere.
$85

253

Pair of English knife boxes in the Adams style.
$1,800

Mahogany urn-shaped knife boxes that are pure Adams. Satinwood inlay. Centennials, but even so, the pair is . . .
$1,750

Traditionally shaped English knife boxes, with interior fittings. For a pair of authentic ones . . .
$2,500

Is the Time of the Primitive Just Around the Corner?

Most New England auctioneers agree that the most undervalued category of the things they sell is primitive American furniture. For one thing, it has not risen in price over the last two decades in the same proportion that other categories, such as Victorian oak and prebandsaw Empire, have. And nobody knows why.

Perhaps it is because each piece is so unique that a buyer has to rely on his own judgment as to whether each piece is a good piece or not, whereas with Empire, for instance, the buyer can compare a piece he is considering to another one whose value has already been established.

These primitive pieces were often made by a farmer for members of his family—a high chair for his son or a dowry chest for his daughter. But chairs and tables and beds were most often made by the local carpenter to fill his time during stormy days or freezing winter months. And he made his pieces to look as much like "city-made" furniture as he could—usually with charming results. But their prices won't go up until buyers become more sure of their own taste. And that trend has already started at the higher-priced level, say these auctioneers. With items such as carved eagles, trade signs, weather vanes, fence decorations, and portraits by itinerate artists already zooming, the time of the primitive may be just around the corner on the lower levels, too.

Nautical Items

Large ship model.
$550

Shadow box with ship
model.
$275

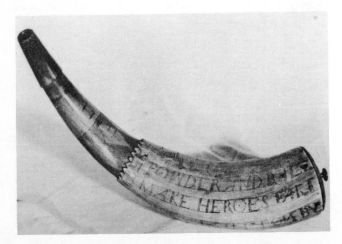

Early scrimshaw powder horn.
$650

256

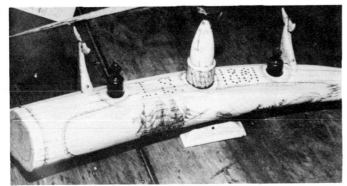

Scrimshaw writing stand, including bottles and pen, dated 1861. If it wasn't a recent fake, it would be worth many thousands of dollars. However, even as a fake it is worth . . .
$1,000

Detail of fake scrimshaw desk set shows the amazingly good craftsmanship of the faker. A lot of this around, and only real experts in the field can detect it.

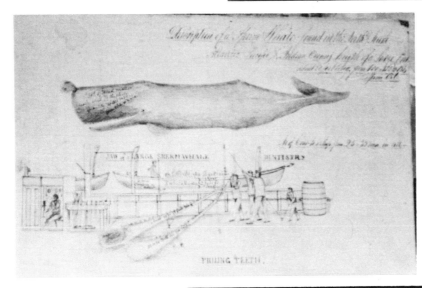

Early pen-and-ink drawing detailing the removal of whale teeth. Circa 1840.
$400

Pen-and-ink drawing to illustrate different types of whale. Circa 1840.
$400

257

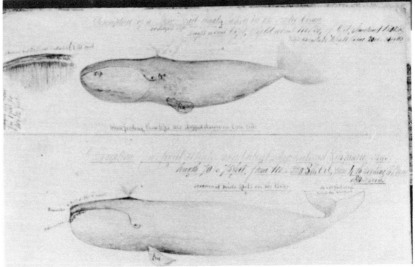

Paintings and Prints

Amateur artist's seascape from early 1900s.
$25

Oil painting from Victorian era.
$1,100

Hudson River landscape, painted around 1880. Hudson River School paintings worth up to $10,000 if done by recognized artists. But for this primitive attempt . . .
$550

Primitive seascape, done about
1890, in original lemon-gold
frame. Undervalued today at . . .
$250

Very collectible ship painting done
in the 1880s, and worth
around . . .
$1,500

Seascape of a ship in a storm,
painted circa 1880. Undervalued at
around . . .
$650

Representative of an Audubon print, worth about . . .
$450

Pastoral scene of cows at the river, painted and signed by C. T. Pierce.
$700

Watercolor on paper of Mount Vernon, commonly done in young ladies' finishing schools. A common subject.
$700–$900

Classed as a still life, these angels come from Holland. Unsigned, but that's not important with this kind of painting.
$2,500

260

Painting on velvet of an imagined landscape, usually done in a girl's school around the late 1800s. Worth around . . .
$750

Pastoral scene, done about 1860.
$350

Signed hunting scene done about 1880, very collectible.
$400

Oil-on-canvas copy of a Currier & Ives.
$300

Italian oil on canvas of the
story-telling school.
$400

Still life painted in the late 1800s.
$425

Oil on canvas of Portland, Maine,
lighthouse. No signature. Primitive.
$850

Oil painting of sheep.
$250

262

Primitive watercolor on paper
depicting "Chinese Fire Drill."
Circa 1900.
   $850

Details of "Chinese Fire Drill."

263

Oil painting of stagecoach stop.
$850

Detail of stagecoach stop.

Currier & Ives print in its original
frame. Maudlin subject.
$60

264

Pewter

Pewter teapots of various makers, **$200–$500.** (Ones signed by famous makers run to **$2,000.**) Pair of candlestands, **$500;** whale-oil lamps (lower right), **$200–$400.**

Collection of Early American pewter. Teapots on top, **$200–500;** candlesticks, **$400;** plates, **$100;** porringers (across the bottom), **$100–$250.**

For pewter that bears no mark of a special maker, prices are: 8-inch plates, **$5–$100;** inkwell, **$125;** porringers, depending on size, run **$150–$300;** pair of candlesticks, around **$200;** teapots, **$150–$300.**

Finding a Good Restorer

Oh, I know the world is full of nice old gents who refinish furniture in their barns. And most antique dealers do it on the side. But what I'm talking about is if you have a broken leg on a Sheraton tambour desk that you want glued back on without *any* trace of the repair showing. Or if you have a cigarette burn on the top of a mahogany Hepplewhite table.

Believe me, these jobs are far more than a "refinisher" can handle. What you need is what the furniture trade calls a "polisher"—a person who is trained in the fine art of making shellac-stick "burn-ins." These are patches that he blends in with the surrounding area by using "wipe-on" stains that come in about 150 colors. And he can blend these with such skill as to defy detection by the human eye.

And where do you find such a person? Not in the Yellow Pages because they don't need to advertise. But there is one in the back room of every major furniture store. Or for smaller furniture stores, he "comes every Thursday." (Calling on other stores, of course, the other days of the week.) Just ask the manager of the store for an introduction. Don't worry. He'll be nice.

Phonographs

Edison cylinder record player with
morning glory horn.
$375

Edison cylinder record player with
small brass horn.
$375

Phonograph horns. Plain ones, **$75** each; morning glory horns, **$125.**

Group of cylinder record players without horns. Each . . .
$175–$275

Victrola from early 1900s.
$150

Pianos

Ormolu-mounted baby grand piano
made by noted French
cabinetmaker, Linke.
$17,000

Louix XV-style baby grand, ormolu
mounted in the manner of Linke.
Authentic, of the period.
$18,000

Baby grand piano with French
Louis XV legs, but that is about all
you can say for it as far as design
goes. It's awkward. However it
works. So . . .
$1,600

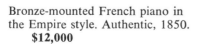

Bronze-mounted French piano in
the Empire style. Authentic, 1850.
$12,000

Portraits

Historically important portraits of
Queen Adelaide and King William
IV—important in Australia. Both
portraits, 5 feet tall. The pair . . .
$12,000

Primitive portrait of a man with a
beard. Oil on canvas. 1850.
$900

Pastel-on-paper portrait of a lady
with an early primitive look and
expressive eyes. Quality.
$1,350

Pastel primitive portrait in
Chinese-type wood frame.
$1,500

Primitive portrait of a young
woman, circa 1830.
$850

Early American primitive portrait
of little girl with basket, in the
manner of Amy Phillips.
$6,000

Nice primitive look in the intense
eyes and writing on the book
makes this painting a real portrait
from the early 1800s.
$1,200

271

Husband-and-wife watercolor portraits with dove of peace between them. Done by a good itinerant artist.
$800

Copy of Gilbert Stuart painting of George Washington, oil on canvas. Good work.
$400

Oval oil painting of mysterious dark-haired woman. Federal period.
$1,100

Portrait of a thinker from around 1840. Unsigned. Done by a craftsman rather than an artist.
$250

Portrait imported from England
to become someone's ancestor.
Done around 1845. Nice Merle
Oberon resemblance.
$450

Ancestor portrait done by a fair
craftsman, 1890.
$150

Oil-painting portrait of a
lost-looking lady. Victorian.
$350

Portrait of man, 1910.
$65

Portrait of woman from 1920s.
$350

Ancestor portrait imported from
England about 15 years ago.
Undistinguished painting, totally
conventional.
$250

Painting for tourists in Spain,
factory produced. There is no
accounting for taste as the old lady
said as she kissed her cow. Goes
for a crazy . . .
$650

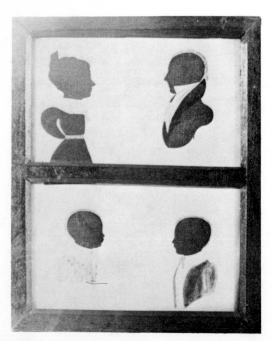

Set of silhouettes. Mom, Dad, and
the kids, unsigned by the cutter. In
original frame.
$1,100

The Psychology of an Antique Dealer

In case you have ever wondered how antique dealers get that way, a recent article in the magazine *Neurosis Today* reveals all:

"The antique dealer is invariably the youngest child in a family of fourteen. This means that in the all-important first six years of his life the older kids are always taking his marbles away from him and he develops an insatiable need to grab anything he can get his hands on. Then in the following juvenile period, while he is strong enough to hang on to his toys, it turns out that they are all hand-me-downs or previously owned objects, used, battered, and broken. And most important of all, objects that were once significant in the lives of other people who came before him. Thus, in his mature years he can only feel inner security if surrounded by objects from the past. *Voila*—you have an antique dealer."

Screens

French Empire screen made up
of reverse paintings on glass of
delicate young ladies.
$24,000

Detail of French Empire screen.

Hand-painted leather screen from
late 1700s.
  $3,500

Teakwood oriental screen made for
a clipper ship. China Trade
period—1870–90 . . .
  $700

277

Secretaries

George III secretary-bookcase. Drawer front falls out to make desk top. Glazed doors, broken-arch pediment, flame mahogany. 1770.
$7,500

Small George III secretary-breakfront. Circa 1780.
$11,000

Georgian secretary-bookcase, circa 1780, with unusually large apron at the bottom.
$4,500

English bureau-bookcase in mahogany, late 1700s. Drawers support lid of desk. Dentil molding on top; French feet.
$4,500

English Chippendale-style bureau-bookcase. Standard stock.
$7,500

William IV secretary-bookcase in mahogany with classical urn inlays in satinwood. Scroll column on plinth base. Some call it Regency, but it ain't. But it has perfect proportions, and is real.
$4,600

English Chippendale secretary, mahogany, 1790.
$6,500

Walnut fall-front desk of the Empire persuasion, 1830–50. Used in office or library.
$1,100

English Queen Anne bureau-bookcase ("secretary" in U.S. usage). Double-dome, blind doors, bun feet. 1740 period, with restorations. Walnut. Because of restoration, only . . .
    $20,000

Excellent 1880 version of a Queen Anne secretary with double dome and mirror doors, burl veneer. The popular small size.
    $4,500

Pine secretary in the Empire mode, circa 1830. Top folds out. Was originally covered with mahogany veneer.
    $1,100

Double-dome Queen Anne
secretary made in late 1800s. Copy
of a 1720 piece. A real one is
$20,000. This one . . .
   $6,000

Double-dome Queen Anne
bureau-bookcase made in U.S. by
a good manufacturer in the 1920s.
Black lacquer.
   $2,500

Queen Anne bureau-bookcase,
single-bonnet top, walnut, 1750. A
lot of restoration as is frequent
with these pieces.
   $18,500

282

Sheraton secretary with blind
doors and a broken arch top.
Fine until you get to the legs,
which are too fat for the rest of it.
1830, pushing price down to . . .
$1,250

Chinoiserie lacquered
bureau-bookcase moving from
Queen Anne into Chippendale
period. Circa 1760.
$16,000

Double-bonnet top Queen Anne
bureau-bookcase, chinoiserie
lacquered, 1740. Some restoration,
of course.
$37,000

Hepplewhite secretary with blind doors. Crotch-mahogany veneer with fair inlay work. Very close to Sheraton period in lines of feet and top. But nice.
$1,800

Hepplewhite desk with a secretary top, made about 1820. Legs and apron in bad shape, but restorable. Super-graceful fretwork on doors in front of single panes of old glass. And since *all* secretaries are good . . .
$2,700

Sideboards

Linke sideboard with ormolu on Louis XV legs. Of the period, authentic.
$11,000

Sheraton sideboard with delicate reeded legs, but no inlay.
$2,000

Large, bulky, gross Sheraton sideboard with bad stumpy legs, clumsy splashboard across the back. A dog at any price, but it is veneered.
$650

Really fully equipped sideboard. Built-in revolving knife boxes, cellarette in lower-left drawer, pull-out regurgitation drawer in right side. (True!) Regency English, 1840. Unique, indeed.
$7,500

Hepplewhite sideboard of good grace. Spade feet on delicate legs the way Hepplewhite should be. Center drawer pulls out and drops to become a butler's desk. Very desirable. About 1800.
$3,500

American-made Hepplewhite style sideboard with nice eagle inlay between center drawers.
$4,500

Small Hepplewhite sideboard with ugly spade feet and brass rail in back for hanging linens. A failure Centennial, but . . .
$1,400

Hepplewhite English sideboard with Adam feeling in decoration. Late 1700s.
$3,700

286

Sideboard made around 1780.
Brass rail in back. Skinny legs.
$3,200

Satinwood-and-mahogany Adams
sideboard. Centennial, but . . .
$4,500

George III Scottish sideboard with
tambour top. Sheraton-Regency
lines.
$4,000

American Victorian golden
oak-period sideboard with mirror.
In original finish, which is as
tough as nails.
$1,600

Elaborate piece of English
Victorian furniture. Sideboard with
mirror top. Fruit carving, 1860.
$3,600

Unbelievable 1860 rococo Revival
American Victorian buffet of oak
with glued-on mahogany carving
and marble top. For the lover of
the different for its own sake.
$3,500

Victorian Renaissance Revival
sideboard with cute French feet,
the rest Italian. Still, undervalued
at . . .
$800

European-made chest of drawers
with marble top. Sheraton lines.
Worth three times U.S. price in
London. U.S. price,
$750

Primitive Sheraton dressing table made about 1820. Painted with false graining and carriage-stripe lined. Pine.
$200

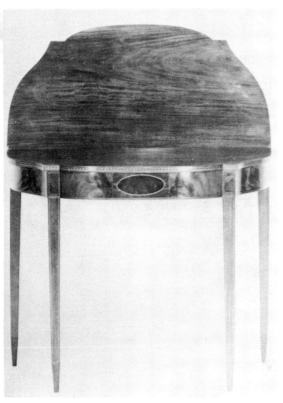

Hepplewhite card table with delicately shaped top and spadeless feet, which is unexpected. Fine inlay and veneering.
$1,700

Sheraton card table with nice inlay across the front. Mahogany.
$1,500

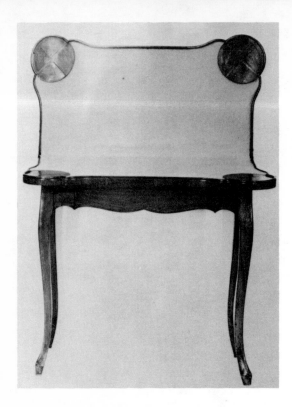

French gaming table in fruitwood, made about 1820. Velvet top with game pockets in the corners. Four of the loveliest Louis XV legs ever made make it look like it's floating. A mere . . .
$1,400

Country Sheraton table with serpentine edge all around the top. Good banderole turnings.
$950

Strange piece that may be a lowboy, but has Queen Anne legs with Spanish-Flemish feet. Sort of impossible. However, wood is nicely stained.
$700

Small painted satinwood server in Hepplewhite-Adams style. Centennial, but very popular.
$1,300

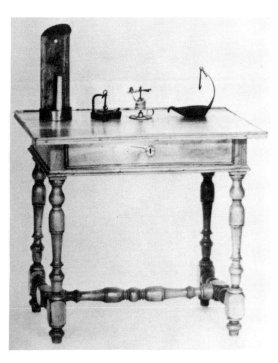

William and Mary style tavern table with bold turnings. Refinished. Replaced top which should have molded edge. But pretty for . . .
$1,200

Satinwood credenza with shelves on top, circa 1800, in Adams style.
$1,200

Oak lowboy in Queen Anne style. (The English call them dressing tables.) Centennial.
$1,200

Super-big server from a Mexican hacienda, greatly restored and decorated with exuberant carving. Hang top, beet feet, and applied carving on the verticals are mostly Empire. 1880.
$900

How to Tell a Fake
(or Detect Restorations)

The difference between a fake and a restoration is that in the case of a restoration a missing piece has been re-created and inserted—whereas in a fake everything has been re-created and inserted. Of course, there is a certain gray area—as when a cabinetmaker starts with a single bedpost and a week later delivers you a whole bed.

At any rate, the main thing is that you have to look at the concealed surfaces of a piece, because regardless of what anyone tells you, any finished surface can be duplicated absolutely, and any joining of wood pieces can be so well obscured as to escape detection by the human eye.

So what you look for is evidence that modern tools have been used on hidden surfaces. Such as smooth, machine-planing inside of cases, and on the underside of drawers. Or the curved marks of a circular saw—which didn't come into use until the industrial revolution. Also, even straight cut lines that are evenly placed indicate that the pit saw was driven by a steam engine—as opposed to the irregular distances between the saw marks that are made by the hand-operated pit saw.

Another give-away of the use of modern machinery is even dovetailing at the ends of the drawers. Roughly speaking, the longer and farther apart the dovetails are, the older the piece. And, of course, screws or any metal braces are a sure sign of recent tinkering.

Even so, if your faker was a real artist (nut), he will have covered his tracks on the hidden surfaces, too. Then you'll need an X-ray machine to detect hidden tool marks inside the joints. Which is what the Ford Museum had to use a couple of years ago to find out that its $19,000 Brewster chair was eight years old.

Stoneware

Product of the Norton Pottery Company of Bennington, Vermont. Perfect condition.
$900

Basket of flowers in cobalt blue on Bennington stoneware. Perfect.
$450

Norton product with Folk-Art bird on it. Perfect. Cobalt blue.
$500

New York-made crock with slip glaze, hand-painted cobalt blue decoration and figure "2" to indicate it holds two quarts of molasses or vinegar.
$250

Group of Bennington stoneware.
Left to right: **$250; $225;** 1853 tall
water cooler, **$1,500; $125; $125.**

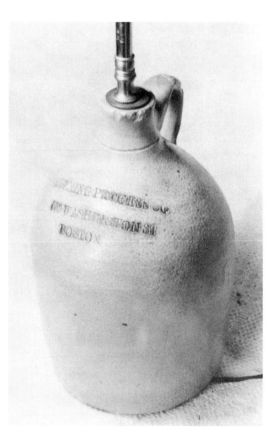

Electrified jug.
$35

Molasses jug to take to the store
and fill from the barrel.
$15

Stools

Centennial example of a good reproduction of a George II or Chippendale footstool. But a lot heavier than the real thing.
$350

Victorian copy of a George I footstool in walnut and gilt. Style of 1730 with paw feet, acanthus leaf on knee, serpentine-shaped top. Unusually good.
$650

Victorian parlor stove with
nickel-plated parts.
$1,000

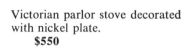

Victorian parlor stove decorated
with nickel plate.
$550

Antiques at Wholesale

Want to see antique furniture on display not by the hundreds of pieces, but by the thousands of pieces? Want to buy furniture and accessories by the truckload? Or maybe just a single piece at wholesale if you don't insult the people by bargaining with them?

Well the giants of the wholesale business are:

Boone's Antiques, Inc., Highway 301 South, Wilson, North Carolina 27893. (Never advertises. It's vast!)

Morton's Auction Exchange, 643 Magazine Street, New Orleans, Louisiana 70190. (Giant warehouses filled row on row!)

Clements Antiques of Texas, Inc., I-20 East of Dallas, Forney, Texas 75126. (High-class things for the Southwest and Southern California.)

Les Freres Beaudin, Inc., Defoy, P.Q., Canada. (Incrediblely large barns full of farmhouse things in the rough.)

Tables

Louis XVI or Directoire table made around 1890. (French Victorian reproduction period.)
$1,800

Gilded eagle console tables from Napoleon's time run about $6,000. This reproduction that can't be dated very well (except that it is not of the period) is worth around . . .
$1,800

Marble-topped console table with mirror underneath, bronze figures. Late Empire . . . Directoire.
$6,500

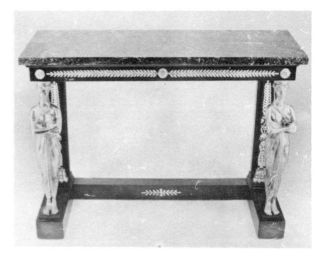

Corner table. When pulled out and squared, it can be used for breakfast or card-playing. 1750.
$1,200

Corner table opened.

Coarse rosewood center table of the American Victorian era. Rococo Revival style. Brown-marble top on mahogany. Worth about six hundred dollars, but selling to the tasteless rich for over . . .
$2,000

Victorian center table made in Europe somewhere. Mahogany.
$1,600

American walnut Victorian center table with marble top.
$850

Baroque Revival Victorian refectory table made in England. Ends pull out.
$1,200

English refectory table in William and Mary style—1680. Centennial.
$2,300

William and Mary-style Victorian oak table.
$450

Oyster-walnut inlaid side or dressing table with tear-drop pulls, William and Mary legs, and brackets that are of questionable authenticity. But very decorative piece, so . . .
$2,600

Chinese teakwood altar table made mid-1800s.
$850

Rococo-carved console table made in France about 1860. Gilded, glazed, and dusted.
$850

French rococo-gilded center table for an exciting lady's apartment. Marble top. Victorian copy of a $24,000 original.
$1,200

Rococo-carved-and-gilded side table in the French manner made in early 1900s.
$850

George I mahogany card table with corner cups. Authentic . . .
$3,800

Gaming table opened.

Late Georgian-style card table with serpentine front and top. Open fretwork is special. Block feet. Centennial.
$750

304

Typical example of French center table made in late 1800s. Kingwood, satinwood. Louis XVI legs that inspired Sheraton style.
$1,400

Envelope or handkerchief table. Four top triangles flip out. Inlaid rosewood. George III style. Centennial.
$700

Sofa table with trestle base in mahogany inlaid with rosewood and satinwood. Edwardian.
$2,400

Sheraton English breakfast table of mahogany with satinwood banding on top. Usual tripod base. 1880s.
$850

English library or writing table made of walnut during the reign of William XIV.
$1,200

Irish Regency table supported by harps. Much higher in London, but here . . .
$2,600

Over a foot has been cut off the legs of this wall table to bring it down to coffee-table height. Typical of the Spanish/Empire blend of styling in the country furniture of Mexico.
$250

Fine primitive table unscarred by
any fake carving. French
influence in corners and legs.
$275

Lovely coffee table made out in the
mountains by chopping the rotted
ends of its legs off.
$150

As popular as ox-bows in Texas is
a table made from the doors of
your granddaddy-don's hacienda in
Mexico. The frame is made of new
wood stained to match the doors.
The turned legs can be new or old.
$895

Cocktail table made from a smallish door—table about four feet long. A couple of old and couple of new legs. Old wood used in frame.
$230

Detail of cocktail table showing old door with an iron spike still in it and old wood frame with channels of worms exposed by recent sawing.

Period Sheraton three-tripod table.
$6,500

Sheraton style two-tripod dining
table made in U.S. Circa 1930.
$1,200

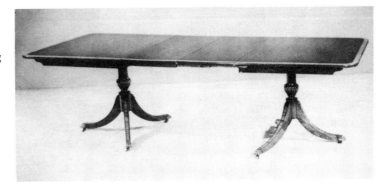

Highly-carved oak dining set.
American Victorian.
$3,400

English red-walnut oval drop-leaf
dining table. Circa 1730.
$1,200

Late George III or Regency
banquet table. In the center a
drop-leaf table with legs, here
swung out to hold up leaves, ends
of which lock onto the two end
tables.
$5,200

Fine rosewood-and-gilt Regency
center or breakfast table.
$4,000

310

Spider-leg drop-leaf table in flame mahogany, circa 1800. English.
$1,000

English Victorian oak dining set including six chairs.
$900

The only thing that is antique here is the hacienda door around which the rest of the table has been built. With six side and two armchairs, this Mexican set goes for . . .
$1,600

311

Tables—Drop Leaf

Made in England Queen Anne
drop-leaf table, shell-carved knees.
Made about 1780.
$2,000

Large Queen Anne drop-leaf table
with maker's mark underneath.
Even with restoration done on the
pad feet (1770) . . .
$3,500

Queen Anne drop-leaf table of
1790 in Honduras mahogany (the
good stuff) with pad feet, round
top.
$2,500

312

English Queen Anne drop-leaf card table. Leaf rises, top twists, and legs pivot out. 1800.
$625

Good Pembroke table with a cross stretcher, some inlay on it, and a drawer. Made about 1820.
$1,200

Hepplewhite Pembroke table with cross stretchers, mahogany, 1800 . . .
$450

313

Sheraton Pembroke with classic
reeded legs, made about 1835.
$450

Country Sheraton drop-leaf with
false graining paint on it. A $200
table with $600 worth of paint on
it.
$800

Molded-leg Chippendale table,
1790. Not a popular design.
$450

Three-part Hepplewhite banquet
table in cherry. Center part is a
drop-leaf table on its own. Ends
can be shoved against the wall as
console tables or up against each
other. Made in 1800.
$3,500

Two-part Sheraton banquet table
with fine delicate legs. Very sought
after for use in an apartment.
Mahogany.
$1,500

Queen Anne tea table with a
shaped apron, cabriole legs,
molded-edge top. Made about
1780. A gem.
$5,000

Birch drop-leaf table with unusual lemon-bulb legs or Sheraton influence. Refinished. Each turning a little different.
$385

Harvest or trestle table in birch, which is hard to find these days. 1820. Call it maple, and who can tell?
$950

Tables—Round

Nice little country-made Hepplewhite table with beaded splayed legs and an oval top.
$800

Shoe-foot hutch table with oval top. Some go to $5,000. This one . . .
$1,200

Ordinary oval-topped tavern table in refinished maple, circa 1800. Not much wear on feet of stretcher base.
$1,400

Round-top hutch table that lifts to make a chair. About 1800. Everybody likes them. This undistinguished one is worth . . .
$650

Good tavern table with a wild base for such in maple. A drawer. 1760.
$3,500

Round-top country-made tea table with red-painted base, scrubbed top, a drawer. A super "the real American thing." Museum quality.
$12,000

318

An English drum table with brass toe casters, drawers all around, tooled-leather top, 1820. (Only four of the eight drawers are real.)
$1,200

Hepplewhite vitrine with glass top and sides, inlay, spade feet. A copy made around 1900.
$400

Rosewood English Regency-Empire breakfast table with scrolled tripod base.
$1,700

English drum table with alternate false drawer fronts. Sloppily executed Sheraton-Regency design. Centennial.
$750

Pair of 1860 American Victorian tables in Renaissance style.
$1,400

Round-top oak dining table on five posts with massively carved feet, weighs a ton. Plus six chairs. Probably $1,500 to $2,000 in New York City. Out in the real world . . .
$750

Tables—Small

Breadboard-top tavern table with red-painted base, bold turning, perfect proportions, original feet. The end of the line—none better. Belongs in a museum.
$14,500

Tavern table with replaced top, but nice legs. Made about 1780.
$750

Reproduction of a butterfly tavern table in curly maple. Note that leaf is planked together with four pieces of wood.
$150

Very, very early tavern table that someone started to clean down on the legs. Queen Anne cutout on the apron, button feet, and breadboard ends on the top. 1760. And worth about . . .
$4,000

Butterfly table that looks like an antique—except it's too perfect. If it were real, $3,500. This medium-good fake . . .
$275.50

Country Sheraton tap table with one drawer, breadboard top. Made about 1800.
$1,200

Hutch table with scrubbed-top with breadboard end, and red-painted base. Made about 1800.
$1,750

Pine, tapered leg table with back drop leaf, 1790–1810. Country Hepplewhite? Pine and maple.
$250

Country-made stand with unusual amount of fluting and detail. Heavy Hepplewhite, made about 1800, in maple.
$350

323

One-drawer Hepplewhite
nightstand. Slightly splayed legs,
board top. 1820.
$275

Country Chippendale tea table
with molded legs, porringer
corners. 1780.
$1,250

Country version of Hepplewhite
nightstand with strange drawer and
a thick, ugly top.
$175

Country nightstand with a bit of a warp to the top. Tapered Hepplewhite legs, nice thin top. 1820.
$250

Delicate Hepplewhite curly-maple nightstand with cut corners, thin top, narrow beaded drawer. Close to the best of it's kind. Note nice warp on top.
$650

Simple Hepplewhite night table with well-tapered legs, cut corners. Shaker look. 1850.
$450

Sheraton nightstand in curly
maple.
$350

Fine birch Sheraton table with
curly-maple drawer front,
cookie-cut corners, thin top. 1820.
$450

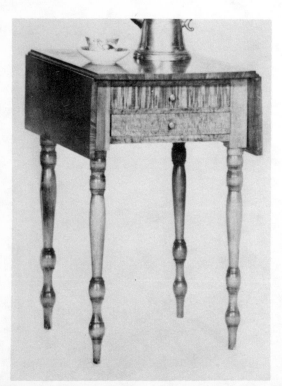

Two-drawer Sheraton nightstand
with drop leaves, graceful turned
legs.
$550

326

Satinwood Pembroke table, painted with fruit and flowers all around. Circa 1790. Adams-Hepplewhite.
$1,600

Sheraton two-drawer lady's worktable with cookie-corner top. Mahogany. 1820.
$450

Oak Victorian side table with marble top. 1880.
$350

327

Tapered-leg stand in maple.
$225

Fine Sheraton tiger-maple,
one-drawer washstand. So
definitely "of the period."
$1,500

Marble-top Victorian walnut table.
$200

Ebony planter of ebonized poplar with boulle inlay in Louis XV tradition. French Victorian era.
$650

Victorian oak plant stand.
$125

Fancy Victorian oak plant stand.
$125

English sewing table made of rosewood in Victorian era after Chippendale design.
$350

Oriental lacquered sewing table of late 1800s. Going begging at : . .
$450

Tables—Tripod

Snake-footed mahogany candlestand, square top. About 1790.
$400

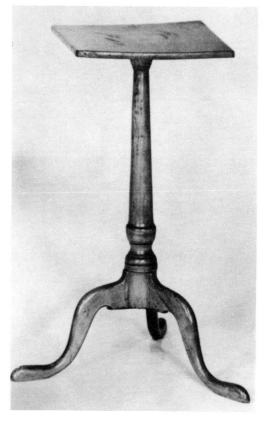

Maple snake-footed candlestand with unusually small square top.
$450

Spider-legged maple candlestand with cut-corner top. 1810.
$450

Maple candlestand with drawer under the top, which is real good, but because the pedestal is so crude, the proportions absurd, and the legs dumpy it is only worth . . .
$400

Maple candlestand made about 1850.
$325

Sheraton tilt-top candlestand with feet cut down, shaped top in some mystery wood.
$300

Serpentine top tip-top table in Honduras mahogany with padded snake feet. 1785.
$1,200

Ugly oak tripod table made mid-1700s.
$750

Round-top table with padless Queen Anne feet. Figured mahogany.
$850

Tripod table with bird-cage support in mahogany. Called a tea table. 1795.
$700

Victorian heavy-legged tripod table of no distinction, except for glued-on edge carving—which could never be—over rounded edge of top.
$450

334

English supper table with spaces
for the plates carved right into
it—Honduras mahogany.
Ball-and-claw Chippendale feet.
Top tilts. Made in 1870s.
(Centennial)
$650

Transitional from Hepplewhite to
Sheraton tilt-top table with highly
figured bird's-eye maple top. 1820.
$475

News of the Auctions
and Antique Shows

The best way to keep up with what is going on in the wonderful world of antiques isn't by reading the slick-covered magazines, but by subscribing to one of the trade papers of the industry.

The most important of these is a tabloid-shaped weekly newspaper, usually running to 120 pages that is published by affable R. Scudder Smith, who is also an important collector. It is called *Antiques and the Arts Weekly,* and the address for subscriptions is: Subscription Department, The Newtown Bee, Newtown, Connecticut 06470. (That's because it was a spin-off from a local newspaper, so, of course, everybody calls it *The Newton Bee* instead of the *Antiques and Arts Weekly,* and if you are confused so am I, and I think they are, too.) Subscription rate is $15 for one year.

But if you are especially interested in Americana, you can't be without rotund Sam Pennington's *Maine Antiques Digest,* which is a *national* "Marketplace for Americana." The address is: Sally Pennington, Maine Antiques Digest, Waldoboro, Maine 04572. Tell her I said she would send you a free sample copy. Subscription $23 a year.

Toys

Early Victorian toy horses.
$125 and **$200**

Carved carousel horse, repainted.
Hershel-Stillman breed.
$1,000

Horse pull toy.
$225

Tin motorcycle toy.
$125

Toy horse on wheeled platform with nice colors and textures not perceivable from photo.
$15

Victorian blocks—set of eight.
$275

Decorative wind-up toy, 7 inches high, lithographed tin, made in Germany. Parasol turns and Woodrow Wilson lifts his hat.
$1,200

Vases

Pair of painted porcelains with
brass ormolu tops and bases from
Germany. 1880s period. The
pair . . .
$1,000

French Empire centerpiece for
dining table, ormolu-mounted
marble.
$6,000

Royal Vienna vase.
$250

Pair of cobalt blue Sèvres vases
with covers, 24 inches tall.
$5,200

Pair of Sèvres vases.
$3,000

Pair of Sèvres urns, cobalt blue,
bronze *doré* plinths. Signed
paintings.
$1,500

Sèvres vase with top and signed drawing-room scene.
$1,200

English painted porcelain urn of the Rockingham period, one of a set. For putting flowers or something in it.
$100

English Victorian vase in manner of Italian Majolica.
$450

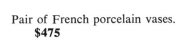

Pair of French porcelain vases.
$475

Japanese Imari vase of late 1800s.
$600

Chinese porcelain jardiniere, 8
inches high. Early 1900s.
$290

Pair of fairly recent chinese vases.
$350

Chinese rose-petal jar on stand.
$85

Chinese rose-petal bowl. China
trade.
$75

Satsuma china vases dating from
around 1910 with nice mandarin
warriors. The pair for . . .
$800

Alabaster vase cut off from
something else.
$75

Part of a garniture set with a
Foo Dog top from the 1890
period. Rose medallion.
$350

Satsumo Japanese cloisonné vase
made 1835, then shipped to
France to be ormolu-mounted
and sold in England or America.
Today . . .
$3,500

Japanese cloisonné vase with
flowers on a bark background.
$450

Three cloisonné vases around 6
inches tall. From left to
right . . .
$75, $125, $150

Imari covered jardiniere. Might
date 1950 as well as 1920s.
$550

Welsh Dressers

Welsh dresser with padded feet
made in late 1700s. Jelly
cupboards on the sides.
$4,500

Welsh dresser with jelly cupboards.
Oak.
$3,500

Welsh dresser with interesting
carved drawer-fronts reminiscent
of Jacobean and base reminiscent
of William and Mary.
$4,500

A weird marriage of the top of a Welsh dresser with jelly cupboards on a nondescript base that is vaguely English.
$3,500

Welsh dresser with jelly cupboards, made of oak in mid-1700s with nice pad feet. The real thing.
$5,000

Welsh dresser or pot cupboard with good fluting at top. Pine, finished with beeswax. Unfortunate phony scalloping on the bottom done by some fool in the 1920s. But still worth . . .
$1,800

Wicker

Fancy wicker rocker, Victorian.
$200

Roll-down wicker rocker in
excellent condition.
$400

Wicker sewing stand with top
missing.
$100

Wicker floor lamp.
$500

Roll-arm wicker armchair.
$250

Wicker sewing stand in excellent condition.
$225

APPENDIX

CRY FAKE!

BY GEORGE GROTZ

Fake antiques are not a joke. They are a crime. Or at least they become a crime the minute you knowingly sell one as the real thing. And you'd better have a signed document to show that you told the buyer that the fake was a fake, or you will have a hard time convincing a judge of your benign ignorance in the matter.

I have learned about such matters by interviewing a famous antiques faker who told me all only after my swearing on his fake Gutenberg Bible not to reveal his identity.

The main problem, he told me, was duplicating the shrinkage of the wood in a genuine old piece. For instance, the round dish-edged top of a three-legged candlestand will have shrunk about a quarter of an inch across the grain, making it a slight oval. This is why you will see many dealers whipping out a tape measure to first measure the diameter of the top with the grain, and then across it.

The same shrinkage should also be found in the central posts of such tables —as well as in all table legs and bedposts. But to detect this you need a caliper. And some dealers carry them, too. (You can get them in any good hardware store that sells carpenters' and woodworking tools.)

Well, the trick, my source tells me, is that after you have made the pieces of your fake, you don't glue them together until you have baked them "loose" in your kitchen oven at 300 degrees for two days. This not only shrinks them across the grain, but darkens the wood to a "natural" antique brown and oxidizes the surface of the wood. This means that the surface fibers of the wood are "cooked"—dried out—about a sixteenth of an inch deep so that when a couple of coats of shellac are applied the wood will have the same patina as if it had been drying out for two hundred years—which is what creates patina in real antique wood.

Another trick is that he doesn't use sandpaper to finish off his surface when making his pieces because that would make them too smooth. He uses scrapers —which is what were used before sandpaper was invented. This leaves a slightly wavy surface that you can sometimes feel when you run your fingertips across a top—or at least see against a low light.

He told me some other things, too, but this should be enough to scare you for the time being. *Caveat emptor!* Even the experts can be fooled. Just ask the Henry Ford Museum and Winterthur. They have special rooms where they keep the fakes that have fooled them—that is, the ones they have detected so far!

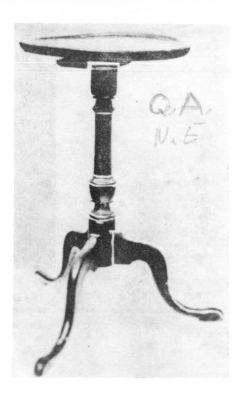

My faker friend found this photograph of a country-made Queen Anne candlestand in a trade publication that reported it had sold for $1,600 at an auction in Maine. He put the white lines on it to get a clearer image when he was enlarging it to make his patterns.

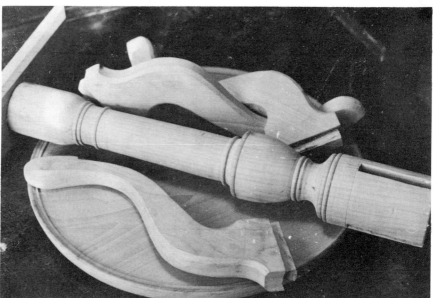

Here are the pieces of cherrywood that he made from his plans—all ready to put in his oven to shrink them across-grain so that the top and column will be slightly oval-shaped. This way he duplicates two-hundred years of natural shrinkage in forty-eight hours. The heat also turns the wood a nice ancient brown, too. (Some people are just lucky!)

Here's the finished stand. Except for a few coats of gloppy shellac that he makes crinkle and crack by a secret process he wouldn't tell me.

On the way out he let me take this photo of the end of his current "production line." Every table is different, of course. After all, if two of the same model showed up, people might accuse him of making reproductions, and he'd be insulted. Anybody can make reproductions —he makes *fakes!*